How They Prayed

Vol. 2—Ministers' Prayers

How They Prayed

Vol. 2—Ministers' Prayers

By Edwin & Lillian Harvey

UNITED STATES ADDRESS
Harvey Christian Publishers, Inc.
449 Hackett Pike, Richmond, KY 40475
Tel./Fax (423) 768-2297
E-mail: books@harveycp.com
http://www.harveycp.com

BRITISH ADDRESS
Harvey Christian Publishers UK
11 Chapel Lane, Kingsley Holt
Stoke-on-Trent, ST10 2BG
Tel./Fax (01538) 756391
E-mail: jjcook@mac.com

Copyright © 2014

Printed in USA
First Edition 1987
This Edition 2014

ISBN: 978-1-932774-77-1

Cover Design by
Isaac Samuel
faithgrafikdesigns@gmail.com

Printed by
Lightning Source
La Vergne, TN 37086

Contents

FOREWORD

A series of articles, entitled "How They Prayed," appeared some years ago in our periodical, *The Message of Victory,* published in Great Britain for over forty years. These were prepared for our reading public by my husband and I, and have been gathered together and enlarged somewhat for this present publication. Our entire purpose is that the reader might be inspired to see the wondrous privileges and possibilities of prayer.

Over the years, we have walked around our spiritual Zion and have noted well her mighty bulwarks, towers, and palaces which, in effect, were men and women who had become convinced that in themselves lay no power or holiness of their own. Therefore they diligently sought unto the Lord, giving themselves to prayer and the ministry of the Word. Thus they became channels through which the unseen God could still make manifest His designs and purposes to their generation. Through their lips and pens poured forth hot words unctionized by the Holy Ghost until the truth of God stood stark and bold against the contrasting fogs and mists of worldly wisdom and materialism.

Then again, we have before us in the Bible pen portraits by the early disciples of our great Exemplar, Jesus Christ, Who did nothing of Himself but what He saw the Father do. He said nothing of Himself, but what He first heard the Father say. He did no deeds of His own initiating, without first ascertaining the Father's will. How completely He set aside His own personal will in order to glorify the Father alone!

If this book could but inspire a few men and women with a like passion to stand quietly in the Father's presence until they, too, could but speak His Words, then the time and effort and money would be well worth the expenditure. Never in the history of the world has there been an era of such great opportunity! May we give ourselves to prayer and the ministry of the Word!

Lillian G. Harvey
July, 1987.

BRIDGE-HEAD FOR THE DAY

"Be thou their arm every morning, our salvation also in the time of trouble" (Isa. 33:2).

"Cause me to hear thy lovingkindness in the morning; for in thee do I trust; cause me to know the way wherein I should walk; for I lift up my soul unto thee (Psa. 143:8.)

"Warrior saints of all time have agreed that the sure way to insure a day of spiritual conquest was to rise early. The early morning hour is the bridge-head of the day's continent which if captured by self-denial for God, gives the soul an advantage over the enemy, obtained by no other means."—Sel.

Mr. Floyd Banker, a missionary to Gujerat, experienced revival in his field of endeavor. He had discovered that the demands upon a missionary are myriad and the tendency is to grow careless in keeping the early morning watch. Mr. Banker shares a secret by which he and his wife learned to conquer where before they had failed:

"Someone may ask, 'What happens when you oversleep or the alarm clock fails? Are there never any exceptions allowed?' I wish to let you into a secret which has become a very simple rule of our lives and is expressed in four little words: 'No prayer, no breakfast.'

"We were brought to this rule early in this new prayer life by a rather strange experience. It so happened one morning that the alarm failed and we overslept. We went out to our breakfast with the thought that we would find time later in the day for secret prayer, but the cares and burdens of our work pressed in and we forgot. The following morning we arose in plenty of time for the prayer hour and each had the same experience. As we went to our separate places of prayer it was as if Christ was already there to welcome us but with a sad countenance as He said, 'I have waited for you twenty-four hours.'

"Like a shock from Heaven this new truth was borne in upon our minds: We had robbed Him of fellowship which He greatly enjoyed.

7

Not only did we benefit from secret prayer but He also received benefit and great pleasure. Do you wonder at our simple rule, 'No prayer, no breakfast?'"—Used by permission as published in the *Wesleyan Methodist.*

In a recent book, *Peace Like a River,* Sallie Chesham tells of the struggle Samuel Logan Brengle had in establishing the habit of early morning rising and the great importance he placed upon this sacred time spent at the opening of a new day:

"Brengle was once asked, 'What are your most feared temptations—the most subtle, the most violent?'

"He answered, 'It is the temptation to start my day for God before spending time in prayer and the Word of God.'

"Before giving this answer however, he held them in a bit of suspense by saying, 'For thirty years I have only had one temptation that has given me any serious concern. But for thirty years, by God's grace, this one has been conquered. So no other has been able to penetrate my armor. But prior to thirty years ago I used frequently to fall before this one temptation; and every time I fell before this one I became instantly vulnerable to ten thousand others.'"

A dangerous time is the morning!
　　There is nothing to fear at night;
Calm are the eyes in closing,
　　Tired of the urgent light;
The body is healed in sleeping,
　　Trouble and labor cease,
The soul is in God's safe keeping,
　　The heart is in perfect peace.

But who can say in the morning,
　　How fierce will the trials be?
What difficult paths may be trodden,
　　What griefs may encompass me?
The whole wide world is sunlighted;
　　But I see not an hour before
What new, strange sorrows or dangers
　　The future may have in store.

O speak to me in the morning,
Lord, of my every day!
Thou art my great Director
As I pass to the hidden way;
If I hear Thy voice in the morning,
I open the day with song,
Forth shall I go to conquer,
Thy presence shall make me strong.
—Marianne Farningham.

"Let each one at all costs observe the Morning Watch," said J. R. Mott, a world-wide, Christian traveler. "What is meant by this habit? It means beginning each day recollectedly with God, in the meditative reading of the Scriptures, in prayer, and in being silent unto God. Notice, the beginning of every day in this way, not every other day, and not simply the days when it is easiest to do so. Most of us have discovered that the days when we find it most difficult to begin in this way are the days when we are most likely to need the particular help which comes from such a practice.

"In the light of experience and observation one may say with conviction that there is no habit more calculated to preserve the sense of reality in faith, to maintain and augment spiritual energy, and to prepare one for recognizing and heeding dangers and opportunities than that of beginning each day in this way."

Many of us owe a debt of gratitude for the help which we have received from the writings of Oswald Chambers. From the following observation by Mr. Chambers' niece we get an insight into his early morning devotions:

"He used to get up very early in the mornings. Sometimes creeping downstairs about 6 a.m. I would find him in the kitchen wrapped up in his plaid, with the inevitable teapot near at hand, reading, writing, sometimes on his knees. Whatever his personal feeling may have been at the sight of his small—and usually talkative—niece, he always had a smile for her, and would fix me up in some corner with a book where I sat important and happy and content just to be with him."

Oswald Smith made the following observation: "For over forty years now I have observed the Morning Watch. I begin by reading the

Word of God, remembering the words, 'As newborn babes desire the sincere milk of the word, that ye may grow thereby' (1 Pet. 2:2). Second, in obedience to Psalm 5:3, 'My voice shalt thou hear in the morning, O Lord; in the morning will I direct my prayer unto thee, and will look up,' I turn to prayer.

"Third, drowsiness. I used to become sleepy when I wanted to pray. That was because I knelt down and closed my eyes, and put my head on my arms. Years ago I formed the habit of walking when praying. By walking up and down the room I never became drowsy. I am able to keep wide awake.

"I discovered that when I knelt down and prayed silently, ten minutes seemed a long time, but when I prayed out loud and walked, the time went by quickly. By following these methods I have been able to spend hours in prayer, *and I have found the morning watch my strength and my stay.* The problems are solved before I meet them. God hears and answers. Instead of letting my circumstances get on top of me and send me to a sanatorium with a nervous breakdown, I am able to keep on top of my circumstances. I know of no greater thrill than the thrill of the morning watch."

There is something inexplicable about the strength which pours into the man or woman who will take the morning watch, not just snatching a hasty twenty minutes or so, but enjoying those quiet, unhurried hours when the unblotted day is fresh and quiet. John Wesley arose at four o'clock in the morning and preached twice each day for fifty years.

Christ set the example when "a great while before day" He was with His Father gaining strength for the day. It was His only time to be alone, for when the morning sun rose, the multitudes would be thronging Him all day long, and His disciples would be desiring His fellowship.

> On the lone mountain side,
>   Before the morning's light,
> The Man of sorrows wept and cried
>   And rose refreshed with might:
> O hear us, then, for we
>   Are very weak and frail;
> We make the Savior's name our plea,
>   And surely must prevail.
>   —Charles Spurgeon.

10

E. M. Bounds, whose books on prayer have brought great blessing and are still being printed, taught some valuable lessons regarding early morning rising to many other ministers. One of these, Rev. Hodge, who esteemed him highly, passes on some of these lessons which are particularly applicable to us in this indulgent age in which we live:

"In the beginning, the physical man revolts against it (early morning prayer); the body, pampered and nurtured for years, refuses to answer to the demands of the soul; the devil will not allow it. Man will not tolerate it. All things in earth and hell protest against it.

"Ninety ministers out of a hundred will tell you it is self-imposed tyranny. O man of God, heed them not! 'Self-indulgence is the law of death; self-denial is the law of life.'

"The family will demur against three or four hours in prayer in the early morning. The powers of darkness are arrayed against you. But be not dismayed. God is near!

"If you miss one morning, your family will know it, and tell the neighbors. Perhaps the very man you have tried to get at early rising will call for you the one morning you failed to rise at four, and find you in bed at six, and call you a hypocrite. Keep patient. God is good and He knows your motives. He forgives when all others condemn.

"My soul for your soul! If you will trust God and really do it, you will realize intense delight. The joy of being with God for hours before the world is awake will fully compensate you for all the trials and sufferings, and the glory you will bring to His name will be inconceivable.

"I do not believe in fads. A man must have a certain number of hours of sleep for his body in a night, and on testing my body I find I must have seven hours and no less, and if I do not get seven hours at night, I get it during the day. John Wesley said his body demanded six and one-half hour's sleep. He got six hours at night and thirty minutes after lunch during the day. But we are trying to follow Christ in praying and have no man in view at all in this matter."

If you have formed the habit of regular, early morning, real praying, and holding to it, you have accomplished about the greatest thing of which a man or woman is capable. Not only do you glorify God and lift others, but you get a good start each day for yourself and you have a splendid start for eternity. It will most surely establish you in God, but to fall here, and keep falling, is to finally fail altogether. Let not

11

him who prays little think he has attained much. Impossible. Prayer is the very breath of spiritual life. Beware of little talks with Jesus when you know the Lord. Little praying is sometimes worse than no praying at all, a sop to your conscience, and an insult offered to your God, Who gave you being, strength, time, and what for?—C. T. Pike.

Did you meet your Lord this morning
　　Ere you saw a human face?
Did you look upon His beauty
　　Through His all-abounding grace?

Did you bow in prayer before Him
　　Ere you went upon your way?
Did you ask for strength to carry
　　All the burdens of the day?

Did you see His will in reading
　　From His Holy Word, and take
Of His promises a portion
　　Blessed with love, for His Name's sake?

Oh, how weak and worthless are we,
　　And our spirits quake within
If we fail to meet our Master
　　Ere the pathway we begin.

How He waits to give His blessing
　　On our lives another day!
Christian, never start without Him;
　　Let Him speak, and then, obey.
　　　　—Union Gospel Press Publication.

BEAT THE DAWN

"Awake up . . . I myself will awake early. I will praise thee, O Lord, among the people" (Psa. 57:8,9).
"Those that seek me early shall find me" (Prov. 8:17).

Through an intensive reading of biography during the preparation of the book, *Royal Counsel,* my husband and I became utterly convinced that those who stayed long in prayer and meditation on the Word were endued with power beyond their fellows. The Bible from that time on had a priority with us it had never had before. We had spent much time with it in our earlier lives, but now we became ardent lovers of the Word. This was because we were inwardly persuaded that there was supernatural strength, both for the physical and spiritual, by perusing the Word in leisure instead of hurrying through our portion for the day.

Those who accomplished much in their personal lives for God in their own particular calling, were those who were up before dawn, preparing their hearts for the happenings of the day. May we help some of you who have perhaps fought a losing battle with this early morning watch. You have tried but been defeated. Let us look at the examples of those who kept this tryst and note their ability to persevere and win through.

As we make a study, a law emerges, namely—that people who have given much time in the morning to prayer and Bible study have always been mighty in their praying, and have succeeded in their labors. That success may not be the apparent kind that all men note, but we can be assured that it will have its reward in eternal consequences.

William Carey's unbroken habit was to begin every morning by reading one chapter of the Bible, first in English, and then in each of the languages, soon numbering six, which he had himself learned. Though an ordinary man, William Carey accomplished much for India by way of translating the Bible into numerous tongues and dialects. The early morning time was doubtless one of the secrets of his colossal contributions to India's spiritual good, for he who gives the Bible to a people, bequeathes a lasting heritage of blessing to a nation.

Ebenezer Erskine, famous in the annals of the Scottish Secession of the Kirk, used to rise at four to pray.

George Whitefield said this of the morning watch: "It is remarked of Old Testament saints, that they rose early in the morning, and particularly of our Lord, that He rose a great while before day to pray. The morning befriends devotion; and if people cannot use so much self-denial as to rise early to pray, I know not how they will be able to die at a stake for Jesus Christ."

It came to my heart with a lesson,
    As the day was beginning to dawn,
As the day, with its cares and trials
    And its blessings, was drawing on,
How Jesus, the world's Redeemer,
    Arose before it was day,
And, feeling His human weakness
    Found in secret a place to pray.

Not even the three disciples
    Who followed the Lord the best,
Were there in His sanctuary;
    They slumbered as did the rest,
And only the stars of heaven
    With, perchance, the silvery moon,
Looked down upon their Creator,
    Who would suffer and die so soon.

If Jesus, the King of glory,
    Commander of hosts on high,
Must petition for daily succor,
    What about such a worm as I?
I rest at ease in the morning,
    Before me a puzzling day;
I know not how I shall meet it;
    But my Savior arose to pray.

How foolish our human blindness!
How hard are our hearts of stone!
Why rise we not in the morning,
And pray to our God alone?
There's help for the daily duties,
And spiritual strength and power,
There's victory for the conflict,
To be gained in the morning hour.

If we walk in the Master's footsteps,
And follow the path He trod,
We must find, in the early morning,
A quiet place with God.
We must pour out our heart before Him,
And let Him into the life,
If we ever shall be the winner
Of victory over strife.
—Minnie Embree Parker.
—In *Biblical Evangelist.*

Barclay Buxton, leader of the Japan Evangelistic Band, wrote to his Christian workers and converts: "Do you rise early? None of us ought to be in bed after six, so that we may have at least one quiet hour with God for prayer and reading of His Word before we meet others, and the day's work begins. At special times we must get more—but no Christian can afford to take less than that."

These missionaries to Japan were given to see sinners transformed by divine grace into saints. Doubtless it was the outcome of the steady vision which was maintained by much aloneness with God.

G. H. Lang became a traveling evangelist all over the world and was greatly used of God. Being British, he was unused to the pace set by American missionaries with whom he at times worked on the field. Listen to what he says: "The life was typically American, one steady rush all day, with visitors, letters, prayer seasons and at nights the meetings in Cairo five days a week, from which we did not return till 11 p.m. City life in England, with its late hour, had caused me to forgo my boyhood's habit of early rising. I now saw that unless it could be resumed there would be no leisure for indispensable privacy with God and soul-nurture. But how resume early rising with days so taxed and retiring so late at night? I besought the special help of the Lord, Who in the days of His flesh had Himself been an early riser (Isa. 50:4; Mark 1:35), and immediately I found myself able to rise at 5 a.m. This profitable practice has continued ever since."

Speaking of early rising, Lang goes on to say: "This used to be easier than it is now. The whole habit of life of the modern world has been changed, and for the worse spiritually, by two inventions, rapid locomotion and brilliant artificial lights. By the latter, night can be turned into day; the world sits up late and cannot rise early. The evident rule of the Creator for His creatures is disregarded by man, and one inevitable result is that while birds and beasts go on without nervous disorders, the human race gets more and more neurotic and undependable."—From *An Ordered Life,* by G. H. Lang, by permission of Paternoster Press, Exeter.

A Christian was once shown over the Lizard Head Lighthouse that stands on the headland marking the most southerly point in Britain. He was ushered into the large room that contained the machinery for operating the fog sirens, after which he was taken up the stairs to the lantern. The lighthouse keeper said something that the visitor never forgot: "We polish the reflectors every morning." "He wakeneth morning by morning, he wakeneth mine ear to hear as the learned" (Isa. 50:4).

John Milton, who gave to the world those marvelous masterpieces, *Paradise Lost* and *Paradise Regained,* arose at four in the morning during the winter, and at five during the summer in order to spend these early hours in writing his immortal poetry.

John Wesley told his preachers that their prime business was to win souls, and that only through unwearied labor and perseverance could they be free from the blood of all men, and he ends thus: "Why are we not more holy? Why do we not live for eternity and walk with God all the day long? Do we rise at four or five in the morning to be alone with God? Do we recommend and observe the five o'clock hour for prayer at the close of the day? Let us fulfill our ministry."

J. D. Drysdale, a man who in our century did much for God in Britain, was an early riser: "For fully forty years," he said, "I have made it a practice to spend the morning watch alone with God. During that time, I have read through the whole Bible every year, following the Murray McCheyne system, which means that every year one reads through the Old and New Testaments once, the Gospels and Psalms twice. Added to this, I have specialized study on different portions.

"In the early morning, I begin to read and become conscious that God, through His Word and His Spirit, is speaking to me, and ere long, I find myself talking to God. How blessed and strengthening to begin the day in this way, to meet with God face to face before we go out to meet the world, to read and digest His Word before we touch our correspondence and the daily paper."

Someone who has done some reckoning regarding this saving of time from sleep to watch with God has noted: "The difference between rising at five and seven o'clock in the morning, for the space of forty years, supposing a man to go to bed at the same hour at night, is nearly equivalent to the addition of ten years of a man's life."

Let us enter into the life of G. C. Bevington, an evangelist God used in America in a remarkable way: "A few weeks ago as I awoke in the morning I felt somewhat under a cloud. A little stiff, I did not seem to be running over with joy, did not hear the joy bells down in my soul. Well, in two or three minutes I saw what I was doing—courting Satan's gloom. It was just 3:30 a.m., my usual time to go to prayer. But instead of going to prayer I jumped out of bed and said, 'Why, good morning, Jesus; glad to see You here.' I shook hands with Him, and set out a chair and told Him to sit down. While I was dressing, washing, and getting my breakfast I just talked out loud to Him just like I would to you were I in your presence. Well, by the time I had all my morning work done and ready to type, I tell you there were no clouds, no stiffness, no gloom, no heaviness, and no despondency. And the joybells were out on dress parade with all their instruments. And I just had to walk the floor awhile under the joys that flooded my soul. Now, I suppose that if anyone would have come along knowing that I was living alone he would have thought me a good subject for the asylum. But we cannot afford to let Satan pile in on us and rob us of our inheritance just because of human considerations."

Mr. Bevington offers some practical advice on how to overcome Satan's wiles in the early morning hour. "When you awaken of a morning you feel quite numb and a little stiff; right here is where you need to practice the presence of Jesus, right on the start before Satan gets in any more of his plans for the day. For if he can get you to look at your feelings five minutes he has you under good headway for a fruitless day. But you at the start go to praising God. But some say, why Brother Bevington, how can I praise God when I am feeling so miserable? Well, we can at the worst find something to praise Him for if we are thus inclined. There is plenty of material to work out a fine display of praise if we look around with our eyes open."

In the quiet of the dawning, alone with Him I love;
The stillness of His presence, brings perfume from above;
It sweetens all the hours of my coming busy day;
Its fragrance calms my restlessness, and drives my fear away.
I find wondrous strength for duty as I look into His face,
And I know that there is power drawn from this secret place.
—J. Charles Stern.

The biographer of Adam Clarke, the commentator, notes his habit of early rising: "It must ever be kept in mind that Mr. Clarke was, from his youth, an extremely early riser, seldom remaining in bed after four o'clock in the morning. Thus he not only availed himself of a considerable portion of the time which many persons consume in sleep, but also of that elasticity of thought which the mind possesses after the rest of sleep, as well as that collectedness of ideas and freshness of feelings, which, as yet, the events of the day have not disturbed. He not only gained time by this system of early rising, but he saved time by rarely accepting any invitations to dinner parties; when he did dine from home, he was almost invariably accompanied by Mrs. Clarke, and they returned home as soon afterwards as possible."

The saintly Samuel Rutherford of Anworth, Scotland, rose at 3 o'clock each morning and his letters and sermons breathe out an intimate love for the Lord Jesus Christ which was gained by this long communion time. "The people that do know their God shall be strong and do exploits."

C. T. Studd also had a habit of early rising and at fifty-two, with disease racking his body, invaded a continent for Christ. His biography, *C. T. Studd, Cricketer and Pioneer*, contains an insight into his usual early morning routine when out in Africa:

"Near the foot of the bed was an open log fire on the dried mud floor. At night, a black form could be seen curled up on a native bamboo couch as close to the fire as he could get, for it was his only 'blanket.' This was his 'boy.' For a number of years the 'boy' was a full-grown man who attended him with the devotion of a woman. He had a stiff leg and so went by the name of 'One-leg.'

"Things would begin to move about 2:30 or 3 a.m. 'One-leg' would wake up as regular as clockwork, and the first sound would be the beating of the sticks together to knock off the burnt ends, and then the long gentle phoo-oo-oo, as he blew the sparks into a flame in the expert native fashion. Then on with the kettle, and soon a cup of tea would be made. By this time Bwana (Studd) would be awake. The tea is handed to him, the boy goes back to sleep again. A Bible is taken down from the shelf, and Bwana is alone with God. What passed between them in those silent hours was known a few hours later to all who had ears to hear.

"At the native meeting in the morning, lasting seldom less than three hours when Bwana took it, at the prayers with the whites at night lasting from 7 to 9 or 10p.m., what he had seen and heard alone with God in the early morning was poured out from a heart ablaze for the salvation of men, and lips which had been touched with a live coal. He never needed more preparation for his meetings than those early hours. . . . He talked with God, and God talked with him, and made His Word live to him."

John Sung, sometimes known as the Wesley of China, was likewise a man who opened each new day with communion with his heavenly Father. Rising between four and five o'clock, he had ample time to steep his soul in the eleven or twelve chapters which he read daily. He neglected all other reading that he might give priority to the living Word. As this man of one Book pressed home Scriptural truth upon his hearers, his preaching was with power.

Sung's biographer, Leslie Lyall, says that "a well-nigh interminable list of his converts and, if possible, their photographs, was his inseparable companion and he prayed for them all regularly, often with tears. Everywhere he went he laid emphasis on the urgent need to pray. That the Chinese Church is a praying Church today can be attributed in part to the influence and the example of this man who prayed."

THE MORNING'S FULL COMPOSURE

"Early will I seek thee: my soul thirsteth for thee, my flesh longeth for thee" (Psa. 63:1).

George Müller has left us his account of how he managed to achieve the early morning rising although he was in bad health when God spoke to him about incorporating this into his life. His account will be of interest to us all when we remember how this man was used of God even to an advanced old age:

"During my stay at Plymouth, I was stirred up afresh to early rising, a blessing, the results of which I have not lost since. That which led me to it was the example of the brother in whose house I was staying, and a remark which he made speaking of the sacrifices in Leviticus: 'Even as the refuse of animals was not to be offered up, so the best part of our time should be especially given to communion with the Lord.'

"I had been, on the whole, an early riser during former years, but since the nerves of my head had been so weak, I thought that, as the day was just long enough for my strength, it would be best for me not to rise early, in order that my nerves might have the longer quiet. On this account I rose only between six and seven, and sometimes after seven.

"For the same reason, also, I brought myself purposely into the habit of sleeping a quarter of an hour, or half an hour after dinner, as I thought I found benefit from it in quieting my nerves. In this way, however, my soul had suffered more or less every day, and sometimes considerably, as now and then unavoidable work came upon me before I had had sufficient time for prayer and reading the Word.

"By the grace of God, after I heard the remark to which I have alluded, I determined that, whatever my body might suffer, I would no longer let the most precious time of the day pass away while I was in bed. By the grace of God I was enabled to begin that very day to rise earlier and have continued to rise early since that time.

"I allow myself now about seven hours' sleep, which, though I am far from being strong and have much to tire me mentally, is quite

20

sufficient to refresh me. In adding to this, I gave up the sleep after dinner. The result has been I have thus been able to procure time for precious seasons of prayer and meditation before breakfast, and thus rest my body and the state of the nervous system in particular; I have been much better.

"If it be asked, but why should I rise early? The reply is: to remain too long in bed is—

1. "WASTE OF TIME, which is unbecoming to a saint, who is bought by the precious blood of Jesus, with his time and all he has, to be used for the Lord. If we sleep more than is needful for the refreshment of the body, it is wasting the time with which the Lord has entrusted us as a talent, to be used for His glory, for our own benefit, and the benefit of the saints and the unbelievers around us.

2. "TO REMAIN TOO LONG IN BED INJURES THE BODY. Just as when we take too much food, we are injured thereby, so it is as regards sleep. Medical persons would readily allow that the lying longer in bed than is needful for the strengthening of the body does weaken it.

3. "IT INJURES THE SOUL. The lying too long in bed not merely keeps us from giving the most precious part of the day to prayer and meditation, but this sloth leads also to many other evils.

"Anyone need but make the experiment of spending one, two, or three hours in prayer and meditation before breakfast, either in his room, or with his Bible in his hands in the field, and he will soon find out the beneficial effect which early rising has upon the outward and inward man. I beseech all my brethren and sisters into whose hands this may fall, and who are not in the habit of rising early, to make the trial, and they will praise the Lord for having done so. Be not discouraged by feeling drowsy and tired in consequence of your rising early. This will soon wear off. You will, after a few days, feel yourself stronger and fresher than when you used to lie an hour or two longer than you needed."

Dr. A. T. Pierson, in his book *George Müller of Bristol,* reveals how the conviction of the importance of prayer grew on Mr. Müller:

"It was in the year 1837 that Mr. Müller, then in this thirty-second year, felt with increasingly deep conviction that his own growth in grace, godliness, and power for service, two things were quite indispensable: first, more retirement for secret communion with God, even at the apparent expense of his public work; and second, ampler provision for the spiritual oversight of the flock of God.

"The former of these convictions has an emphasis which touches every believer's life at its vital center. George Müller was conscious of being too busy to pray as he ought. His outward action was too constant for inward reflection, and he saw that there was risk of losing peace and power, and that activity even in the most sacred sphere must not be so absorbing as to prevent holy meditation on the Word and fervent supplication. The Lord said first to Elijah, 'GO, HIDE THYSELF'; then, 'GO, SHOW THYSELF.' He who does not first hide himself in the secret place to be alone with God, is unfit to show himself in the public place to move among men.

"Mr. Müller afterward used to say to brethren who had 'too much to do' to spend proper time with God, that four hours of work for which one hour of prayer prepares, is better than five hours of work with the praying left out; that our service to our Master is more acceptable and our mission to man more profitable, when saturated with the moisture of God's blessing—the dew of the Spirit. Whatever is gained in quantity is lost in quality whenever one engagement follows another without leaving proper intervals for refreshment and renewal of strength by waiting on God. No man, perhaps, since John Wesley, has accomplished so much even in a long life as George Müller; yet few have ever withdrawn so often or so long into the pavilion of prayer. In fact, from one point of view, his life seems more given to supplication and intercession than to mere action or occupation among men."

Dr. Pierson has also recorded Müller's love for the Word of God. "In his ninety-second year, he said . . . that for every page of any reading he was sure he read ten of the Bible. . . . During the last twenty years of his life he read it carefully through, four or five times annually, with a growing sense of his own rapid increase in the knowledge of God thereby."

> All day, perchance, thy feet must tread the valley,
> All day the multitude around may throng—
> With claims unceasing, pressing close upon thee,
> And voices loud in sorrow, strife, or song.
>
> Before the multitude, before the valley,
> Before the toil that binds thee, heart and hand,
> Be ready, in the first, fresh hour of morning,
> High in the mount, alone with God to stand.

What then? O He is waiting there to meet thee—
Himself in strange, sweet beauty to reveal;
Himself with thee alone to hold communion—
To lift thee past earth's shadows to the Real.
—E. H. Divall.

William Bramwell, a man mightily used of God in England, had very firm convictions concerning early rising for prayer and Bible reading. "His general custom was to rise at four in the summer, and five in the winter. If he was at any place where people began their work at an earlier hour, he would rise earlier, unless prevented by indisposition, as he could not bear the idea of anyone being occupied in worldly business before he had engaged in the service of the heavenly Master. The time thus redeemed from sleep he diligently devoted to prayer, reading the Scriptures, and study. He found that those days which were commenced with importunate prayer were spent in joyous praise and thanksgiving. Generally his plan was, after some time spent in earnest prayer, to read one or more chapters in the Bible, and then again approach the Throne of Grace. These alternate exercises were repeated several times early in the morning. He used to say, 'I like to have my soul filled with God in the morning, and then I am in the Spirit all the day.'

"Several of his friends with whom he lodged in the country witnessed, when he left his room in the morning and came to breakfast, that his hair was bedewed with perspiration as if he had been engaged in the extremity of manual labor. These efforts produced their natural results, and such a wrestling Jacob became a prevailing Israel.

"He often rose at midnight for prayer, and has been sometimes found by his friends who had overheard him on his knees, wrapped in a blanket engaged in this delightful exercise."

Writing to a friend he advised, "O how Satan will tempt you to lie in bed these cold mornings, when you should be engaged in prayer, and in your study every morning at five o'clock or before. By this practice what wonders you would do with God, with the Word, with your soul, and for your family."

Again he wrote, "If you receive what I call 'the full composure' in the morning, the mind stayed upon God, the solid rest, this will carry you into all your little concerns with the utmost patience, and the daily cross will be the blessed means of increasing your heaven. And this is a constant heaven; this is your place—to have God your all."

A man with such consistent prayer habits was bound to see the power of God working through him in very ordinary circumstances. His prayer for a blind boy as he was about to depart issued in a miracle of healing which today would be heralded all over. It seemed to Mr. Bramwell the only thing to be expected when it was God's purpose. We quote the instance taken from *Striking Incidents of Saving Grace,* by Henry Breeden:

"When William Bramwell traveled in the Nottingham Circuit, he always stayed at Mr. Greensmith's house for the night, when he had preached in the neighborhood of Watnall. And the last time he was at that house, before he removed from the Nottingham Circuit, the following wonderful cure took place.

"Having slept there during the night, and Mr. Greensmith having gone very early to his labor, Mr. Bramwell took breakfast the following morning alone, only Elizabeth and the two boys being at home. After breakfast, the Minister prayed with the children in the way of family prayer. And that being his last visit, he prayed very earnestly for them. Then, having got all ready, he prepared to mount his horse and go on to his next appointment. But before doing so, he said, 'Where is the blind boy?'

"To this it was replied, 'He is behind the door.'

"Then William, on coming out of the cave stepped towards Mr. Bramwell, who just then laid his hand on the blind boy's head. He stood in that posture for some time, in deep mental prayer, occasionally giving a very deep groan. Having at length concluded prayer with the boy, he shook hands with him and the other two, and then going towards the door, near which his horse was standing, he mounted and set off on his journey.

"He had scarcely gone from the door, when the blind boy cried out with a loud voice, 'Oh! Our Bess! Where is Mr. Bramwell? I can see! I CAN SEE! I CAN SEE!' And then, all the three young people began to shout and run in amazement after the man of God, crying aloud, 'Mr. Bramwell! Mr. Bramwell! He can see! He can see! I can see! I can see!' Then the good man waited to hear their account, and rejoiced with them, after which he again blessed them, and departed.

"And Wm. Greensmith, the once blind boy, whom I knew intimately for nearly fifty years, lived afterwards at Harrogate until he was about eighty years of age, and ever had the best of sight, up to his dying day!"

Yet never sleep the sun up; prayer should
  Dawn with the day: these are set awful hours
'Twixt Heaven and us: the manna was not good
  After sun-rising; for day sullies flowers:
Rise to prevent the sun; sleep doth sins glut,
  And Heaven's gates open when the world's is shut.
                                        —J Henry Vaughan.

John Eliot, a very early settler in New England, was greatly used
among the North American Indians. Cotton Mather wrote of the early
morning exercises of this missionary pioneer: "The sleep that he allowed
himself cheated him not of his morning hours but he reckoned the
morning no less a friend unto the graces than the muses. He would call
upon students, 'I pray, look to it that you be morning birds.' And for
many more than a score of years before he died, he removed his lodging
into his study, on purpose that being there alone, he might enjoy his
early mornings without giving the disturbance of the least noise to any
of his friends, whose affections to him else might have been ready to
have called, 'Master, spare thyself.'"

              O brothers; in these silent hours
              God's miracles are wrought;
              He giveth His beloved in sleep
              A treasure all unsought.

              I sit an infant at His feet,
              Where moments teach me more
              Than all the toil and all the books
              Of all the ages hoar.
                                  —Tersteegen.

ENGLISH PREACHERS

"I have studied the Bible and history with extreme care, and wherever I have found a man of power I have found a man of prayer," was the profound conclusion of the Bishop J. C. Ryle. Our own diligent study into religious biography has likewise convinced us that men and women of the past and present who have made and are still making a lasting mark upon their generation were and are, always and everywhere, people of prayer. They disturbed the devil's kingdom; they wrought righteousness; they brought the Kingdom of God into being, dislodging the kingdom of darkness—all through prayer. Even the most prayerful of people today are made to feel quite content if they compare their devotional life with the meager scraps of time given by the majority of evangelical Christians to the Lord Whom they profess to serve.

The fact that we are failing to make any impression upon the appalling statistics of crime, drink, immorality, lawlessness, and violence, gives a lie to the claim that we are producing the kind of converts in any number who, like the early church, turn the world upside down. Could God be God, and give to our present-day, light-swinging, entertaining type of evangelism the supernatural assistance that men of the past obtained by travail and soul agony, violence in prayer, and efforts of self-denial? Some laugh at this type of seriousness and believe that only by becoming like the men of the world whom we seek to win will we be successful. God's character does not alter to suit an adulterated Christianity.

The healthiest thing we can do is to study the prayer lives of fruitful soul-winners. How did they pray? How long did they pray? Regardless of our profession, let us not fear to measure alongside them our own meager praying, even though it causes us to come to repentance and tears.

George Fox

The Quakers were a praying people. William Penn said of George Fox, "Above all, George Fox excelled in prayer. The inwardness and the light of his spirit, the reverence and solemnity of his address and behavior, the fewness and the fullness of his words have often struck even strangers with admiration as they were used of God in bringing light to the hearers. The most awful, living, reverent frame I ever felt and beheld, I must say, was his when in prayer. He knew and lived nearer to the Lord than other men."

Could the walls of the English prisons have recorded the out-breathings of the many maligned Quakers, who passed years of their lives in these unhealthy holds and yet kept their faith in God, we would have a mighty record of prevailing prayer.

Joseph Alleine

The Puritans, too, were an exceedingly prayerful people. Joseph Alleine, who wrote his *Alarm to the Unconverted* while in prison, was expelled from his home and pulpit during the fearful time in England when over 2,000 ministers refused to bow down to the State but remained true to God and their inward persuasions. Alleine literally breathed the atmosphere of another realm.

"Though I am apt to be unsettled and quickly set off the hinges," he tells us, "yet methinks I am like a bird out of the nest; I am never quiet till I am in my old way of communion with God, like the needle in the compass that is restless till it be turned toward the pole. I can say, through grace, with the Church, 'with my soul have I desired thee in the night, and with my spirit within me have I sought thee early.' My heart is early and late with God; 'tis the business of my life and the delight of my life to seek Him."

"He poured out his very heart in prayer and preaching," his biographer said of him. "His supplications and his exhortations were so affectionate, so full of holy zeal, life, and vigor, that they quite overcame his hearers; he thawed and mollified, and sometimes dissolved the hardest hearts."

His wife remarked that when he was in good health, "he did rise constantly at or before four of the clock, and would be much troubled if he heard smiths or other craftsman at their trades before he was at communion with God, saying to me often, 'How this noise shames me. Does not my Master deserve more than theirs?' From four until eight he spent in prayer, holy contemplation, and singing psalms, in which he much delighted and did daily practice alone as well as in the family. Sometimes he would suspend the routine of parochial engagements, and devote whole days to these secret exercises in order to which he would contrive to be alone in some void house, or else in some sequestered spot in the open Valley. Here there would be much prayer and meditation on God and Heaven."

Charles Simeon

Then there were godly Church of England ministers such as Charles Simeon, a deeply spiritual man. His biographer states: "Invariably Simeon arose every morning, though it was the winter season, at four o'clock, and, after lighting his fire, he devoted the first four hours of the day to private prayer and the devotional study of the Scriptures. He would then ring his bell, and calling in his friend with his servant, engage with them in what he termed his family prayer. Here was the secret of his great grace and spiritual strength. Deriving instruction from such a source, and seeking it with such diligence, he was comforted in all his trials and prepared for every duty.

"This early rising did not come easily to him; it was a habit resolutely fought for and acquired. Finding himself too fond of his bed, he had resolved to pay a fine for every offence, giving half-a-crown to his servant. One morning, as he lay warm and comfortable, he caught himself reasoning that the good woman was poor and that the half-crown would be very useful to her. But that practical fallacy was not to be tolerated; if he rose late again, he would walk down to the Cam and throw a guinea into the water. And so he did, though not without a great struggle, for guineas were not abundant in his purse, and also he had learned to look on them as 'his Lord's money.' But for his Lord's sake the coin was cast in, and there it lies, yet, no doubt, in the river's keeping. Simeon never transgressed in that way again.

"An attic window, lighting other rooms, opened upon a path, but in Simeon's time this was never used; and the old man's heavenly Master alone can tell how often he paced that narrow way confessing, petitioning, consulting, praising, adoring. If I do not mistake, those leads were often wet with his tears, and often pressed by his knees as he paused for some special act of worship; for no man ever felt more deeply than Simeon did the blessedness and duty of adoration. He loved to speak of that great vision of the prophet, where the six winged Seraphim 'fly twain,' but with four wings veil themselves before the eternal glory. . . ."

Henry Martyn, his devoted convert, said of Simeon: "Never did I see such consistency, and reality of devotion, such warmth of piety, such zeal, and love. I owe that great and holy man a debt which cannot be cancelled." India owes Simeon a debt of gratitude for giving her such a devoted missionary and Bible translator as Henry Martyn.

John Wesley

John Wesley was also a Churchman, who, though he led the Methodists, never did leave the bosom of the Church of England. For prayerfulness and zeal, it is difficult to find his equal. Wesley did not think much of a Christian who did not spend at least four hours in prayer every day.

In his own diary we find the resolve: "To dedicate an hour, morning and evening; no excuse, reason, or pretence; to pray, EVERY HOUR, seriously, deliberately, fervently." And throughout his life he did not mitigate this resolve. For over forty years, day after day, his diary begins by the word "prayed." It ends with the act of prayer, and during the daily record he thought it of enough importance to record prayer four, five, or even six times daily. In his abundant travels which involved much visiting, he would deny himself mere social intercourse which can eat up hours of priceless time; he allowed himself only one hour, and then it was of so spiritual a nature that it often resembled a class meeting.

He was perhaps the most retiring of men in his time in spite of his multitudinous public duties. He said that by his rides he was "as much retired ten hours a day as if he were in a wilderness." And thus few persons spent as many hours secluded from all company as he. Even so, in order to obtain more time alone, he rose at four o'clock in the morning.

John Fletcher

The Rev. John Fletcher, a member of the Church of England and a close associate of Wesley, became attached to the Methodists because of this very quality—their prayerfulness. His first introduction to them came in an unusual manner. Rebuked by his landlady, Mrs. Hill, for copying music on the Sabbath evening, he became more earnest in his attention to religious duties. One day, Mrs. Hill declared she wouldn't wonder if Fletcher turned Methodist. "Methodist, madam," he exclaimed, "pray what is that?"

"Why, the Methodists are people who do nothing but pray; they are praying all day and all night," replied Mrs. Hill.

"Are they?" said Fletcher, "then, by the help of God, I will find them out, if they are above ground." Little wonder that Fletcher became one of the godliest men of his time. During a period of a few months, he poured out such supplications and entreaties that the walls of his study bore witness to his burden and were stained with the breath of his supplications.

His wife came from a wealthy family, and although, like her husband, she never left the Church, she assisted Wesley in the promotion of Methodism. She says: "I long for close communing. My soul pants after it. I have wonderful answers to prayer. This evening I spent two hours in retirement, and found it the best of all the day. God give me a praying spirit." And again she writes, "I have found it three years of prayer. Never did I know three years of such suffering, and never did I know three years of such prayer."

John Nelson

Reading the annals of the early Methodist Church you will find she produced a praying people. A praying leader begets praying preachers and laymen.

John Nelson, one of Wesley's assistants, said, "If you spend several hours in prayer daily, you will see great things." He made it a rule to get out of bed at midnight and sit up till 2 a.m. for prayer and converse with God. Then he slept until 4 a.m. at which time he always arose for the day. We might well say with L. M. Montgomery, "Isn't it a splendid thing that there are mornings."

William Bramwell

William Bramwell went through England a veritable flame of fire. Souls were won by the thousands, but behind the scenes there was wrestling and agonizing prayer. His biographer says: "He spent hours in prayer. He almost lived on his knees. The fire was kindled by the time he spent in prayer. He often spent as much as four hours in a single season of prayer in retirement."

"After twelve hours of groaning and using every means, God has opened blind eyes. I never saw the power of God more visibly displayed: whatever may be the effect, it was God Who produced it."

He diligently sought renewed baptisms of the Holy Ghost by fasting and prayer. "I am drinking much deeper into its spirit; and in praying without ceasing I shall receive the fullness of God. I am more than ever ashamed of unbelief. Oh, how it dishonors God and His truth!

"I see more than ever that those who are given up to God, in continual prayer, are men of business, both for earth and Heaven. They go through the world with composure, are resigned to every cross, and make the greatest glory of the greatest cross. On the other hand, if not given up to God in prayer, every cross brings the greatest perplexity, and robs them of the little love and patience they enjoy. To be all alive to God, is as it were two heavens; to be unstable and not a whole Christian, is two hells."

In advice to another minister he says: "O, my brother, resolve to rise early; let not flesh and blood hinder; gain this point, and all will fall beneath your feet." To another he writes: "Continual prayer will bring the grace for this purpose. Knock often, knock hard, and come boldly. Do not say, 'I have been, morning and night'; but several times, yes 'seven times a day call upon Him.' Oh this prayer—this faith—this God—this Heaven!"

He shares his struggles with us: "My warfare is continued. I am surrounded with the powers of darkness. My temptations to sloth, to fainting, against preaching and praying are as great as ever, and I think are much increased. Invitations to feast with many of the friends who are in superior situations, and are naturally friendly, are more numerous in this place than I have ever known, and have a tendency to produce these effects."

And so he denied himself long conversations with men. And when he did converse, he left politics to the politicians and business to the merchants, but pressed home to men and women the soul's importance and their need of God—NOW!

A man who stayed with Bramwell at the same residence said: "He was wont to resort to it (a special room), and spend two, three, four, five, and sometimes six hours in prayer and reflection. He often entered the room at nine o'clock in the morning, and did not leave it till three in the afternoon. The days on which his longest visits occurred were, I conjecture, his appointed fasts: on these occasions he refused any kind of refreshment, and used to say when he came in, 'Now take no notice of me.'"

John Smith

"God will do astonishing things for others in answer to our prayers," said the saintly John Smith, a minister used in an outstanding way in England during the first part of the nineteenth century. Few men have attained the spiritual stature which this man of prayer did. When objections were raised by his fellow-ministers as to his lavish expenditure of strength, he wept at their loving remonstrances as he told them that the value of one human soul weighed so much with him that no consideration of length of life, wife, or children could possibly induce him to curtail his arduous and strenuous efforts for the salvation of such souls.

In a biography of John Smith, Richard Treffrey gives the reader a fleeting glimpse of the hours this man spent in prayer:

"His times of family worship were often seasons of most gracious effusions of divine favor. 'We had a blessed baptism of the Spirit last night at family-prayer. We have devoted ourselves afresh to God, and He accepts us.' It was especially when the members of his family accompanied him to the Throne of Mercy that the piety of the husband, the father, the master, and the friend was presented in its most impressive and touching aspect. Mr. Smith's pertinent observations on the portion of Scripture (the reading of which formed a regular part of the service), the singular sweetness of the family music, succeeded by powerful and appropriate prayer, could not fail to affect a mind endowed with any measure of religious feeling.

"After family worship of the morning, which Mr. S. usually prefaced by several hours of private devotion, he returned to the exercises of the closet, and sometimes on his knees, and often on his face, wrestled with God, till not infrequently a considerable part of the floor of his study was wet with his tears. In his unreserved disclosures of feeling to his friend, Mr. Clarkson, he once remarked that he was sometimes engaged in prayer for two or three hours before he enjoyed that unrestricted intercourse with heaven which he always desired, and which he generally succeeded in obtaining.

"'Often,' says another of his friends, 'when I have gone to his house with those who were seeking salvation, I have interrupted his devotions, in which he would be engaged for seven or eight hours at a time. He occasionally spent the whole night in prayer; sometimes the greater part, if not the whole, of several successive nights. And when he has been from home, the members of the families by whom he has been entertained have, at various hours of the night, been awakened by his groans, when his desires became too big for utterance and his emotions too mighty to be controlled.'

"Of his public and social prayer, perfectly simple and inartificial as they were, multitudes have testified that the Divine influence attending them exceeded anything which they had ever experienced. The author of these pages, in common with many others, has seen persons so affected under them, that nature itself has sunk, and they have been removed from the scene of action in a state of insensibility."

Once when preaching at High Wycombe circuit, the congregation had assembled on the Sabbath awaiting the preacher, John Smith, but he was nowhere to be found. After a lapse of time, they found him in a secluded place out-of-doors, so completely absorbed in his intense soul-wrestling that, oblivious of the passing hours, he had completely forgotten his appointment. It was little wonder that souls were blessed, justified, and sanctified. Everywhere he went, results followed in the wake of his efforts. But the human frame could not long withstand such intercessory demands, and at the early age of thirty-seven he died still entranced with the thought of the worth of souls and the greatness of Redemption. Oh God, give Thy Church more men like these!

33

Samuel Bradburn

Samuel Bradburn was another of Wesley's preachers and finally became the president of their Conference. The private out-breathings of his soul reveal the man: "I blame myself in many things, particularly for not living more in the soul of prayer. But I bless God for my seeing this, and for feeling a revival of it at this hour and a determination to begin again." In an exhortation from his spiritual superior, he is advised: "Remember your business is to save souls, and that if this end be not answered, your reading, praying, studying, and preaching will turn to poor account. Spend at least eight hours every day alone."

John Oxtoby

John Oxtoby was just an ordinary man when it came to the matter of personal endowments of intellect or talent, but in prayer he was a giant. One who was stationed with him on the Halifax, (England), circuit says: "During the time of his stay at Halifax, he was much given up to prayer, and generally spent about six hours each day upon his knees, pleading earnestly with God on behalf of himself, the Church, and sinners, whose salvation he most earnestly desired." When confronted with some unusual problem, or stubborn field, he would resort to prayer, sometimes for whole days and nights. God could not but answer such importunity, and whole audiences bowed beneath the might of the Spirit.

Thomas Champness

Thomas Champness, one-time editor of *Joyful News,* the organ of Cliff College in England, knew much of the prayer life. He had stepped forward in a faith venture and started a six-month's training course for laymen who desired to minister for God but who, because of home commitments or financial obligations, could not enter into full-time ministry. It evolved into what became a well-known institution in England called Cliff College. "I feel," he said, "except Methodism will pray we must submit to loss. Prayer that can make sacrifices and be more or less in agony and travail, prevails. . . . I am not sure that the brethren liked my saying that self-denial opened the lips of the Holy Ghost, and self-indulgence closed them. But it is true!"

Again this prayer-champion remarked, "A plain man once said in the presence of the writer, 'You must get up soon of a morning if you intend to get to windward of the Almighty.' He spoke the truth."

Samuel Chadwick

Samuel Chadwick, also mightily used of God and one-time president of Cliff College, had frequent times when bodily weakness compelled him to take a rest from his heavy labors. "Sleepy Hollow," he called these rest times, where he unfailingly was given further vision to be worked out when he returned to active ministry.

"There have been times," he wrote, "when I have crept into the Hollow by stealth, and many times I have laid a firm hand upon myself, and turned back like one caught unawares. As I grow older my reproach is that I have not allowed myself to roam and dream as much as I ought. If I stood at the Judgment Seat tomorrow I should have no reproach of idle days. Whatever else I have done or left undone, I have worked. I do not wish I had done less, but it would have given strength and serenity to have had a lodge in the Sleepy Hollow of the wilderness."

At a conference where he ministered he wrote: "It has been a happy time. Yet, having here but limited opportunity for secret reading and prayer, I feel the lack, and long to reach home. For me, sermons and public exercises are not enough. I never prosper without much retirement."

From a lad Chadwick had begun the habit of prayer. Three times daily he went aside to pray. But later, when reviewing seven barren years of preaching and when he had come to the end of what eloquence and logic could do, he betook himself to prayer. Soon thirty or forty people signed a covenant to pray daily for a revival of God's work.

A diary entry reveals a typical day in his life. "Six hours this day I dedicate to acts of devotion." Again, "The answering hand of God waits for the lifted hand of man, and the heart that answers always transcends the heart that cries."

"I believed," said Chadwick, "that when a man talked to God, God talked back; and when He talks to a Lancashire lad He doesn't talk Dutch. . . . How I looked at those great, strapping fellows at the public house corner, abandoned by Church and friends as hopeless, and longed for their salvation." Then revival came. The wicked men bowed. "Fire came down in answer to believing prayer, and earnest, dogged work for the salvation of men."

At one of his appointments at Orkney, his lodging furnished him with no vocal freedom in prayer. His biographer tells us how he managed to find a secluded spot in a sheltered cave in a cliff. "Though he knew it not, loving people observed his frequent resort thither, and wonderingly found that their evangelist often spent successive hours communing with God in that cold closet on the shore. Sometimes a whole day passed in fasting, intercession, and meditation."

His advice to a young minister is well worth pondering: "Get your sermon preparation well done before the Sabbath; turn into bed in good time on Saturday night, and out of it early on Sunday morning. Get three hours with God before you go to the pulpit; get at Him by reading, believing, and praying over His Book. Talk with Him till He talks with you and says, 'Go in this thy strength.'"

We close this brief glimpse into Samuel Chadwick's prayer life with some poignant words written in his more mature years:

"To pray as God would have us pray is the greatest achievement on earth. Such a life of prayer costs. It takes time. Hurried prayers and muttered litanies can never produce souls mighty in prayer. Learners give hours regularly each day that they may become proficient in art and mechanism. All praying saints have spent hours every day in prayer. In these days there is no time to pray; but without time, and a lot of it, we shall never learn to pray."

Since Samuel Chadwick wrote these directives to prayer, the Church has drifted a long way from her original moorings. Hurried prayers are much more in vogue today for the get-going preacher who often holds down a job while he preaches and oversees the many social functions in the Church. Or if he is not working, he has so many appointments and so many fingers in the pie that he has little time for those long, meditative times "when God comes down the soul to greet, and glory crowns the mercy seat."

MORE ENGLISH PREACHERS

"It is pathetic what a time God has getting a hearing down here. He is ever speaking, but even where there may be some inclination to hear, the sounds of earth are choking in our ears the sound of His voice. God speaks in His Word. The most we know of God comes to us here. This Book is God in print. It was inspired, and it is inspired. God Himself speaks in this Book. That puts it in a list by itself, quite apart from all others. Studying it keenly, intelligently, reverently, will reveal God's great will. What He says will utterly change what you will say."

The above words were spoken by S. D. Gordon who wrote quite a bit on the subject of prayer. We agree that the reading and meditating on the Word of God is one aspect of prayer. We so often go to Him like a babe or carnal Christian, requesting things for ourselves. Parents spend much time, when their children are little, just supplying their needs. "Mummy, where's my school bag?" "Mummy, I bumped my head." "Mummy, I've hurt my finger." "Mummy, I can't find my bat." "Daddy, I need some money." "Mummy, I've got my exams today, will you pray for me to get through?" What a wonderful day it must be for those parents when their child matures and in gratitude sits down with them, and, instead of the expected asking for something, he or she says "Look, Dad and Mum, I know you've had financial burdens, and your business problems are great. Is there any way that I could help?"

So many Christians never grow up, and they are forever asking. They do not realize that the Word says that Christ is Lord of the Harvest. He knows the ripest place to reap. But we run about trying to reap His harvest, perhaps ever so sincerely if mistakenly, and He allows us to do so until we, tired of our ineffectual efforts, come to the Lord God of harvests and ask for direction. Previous to that it is ever, "Bless the service I am about to take. Bless this endeavor we are making." Bless, bless, bless! Me, me, me, me, or us, us, us, us!

True prayer is spending much time in reading the Word of God to find out what pleases our wonderful Savior, and then asking that we might be permitted to extend His kingdom in His way instead of in our childish fashion, and with such limited vision. God is so patient with His children, but we wonder if He is not often grieved at heart to find so few truly interested in His concerns.

You might say, "I'm in full-time Christian service. Aren't those interests His?" Not necessarily. Ambition, desire for success, and hope of fulfillment are natural elements which often figure greatly in our prayers, and we may well ask amiss that we might consume it upon our own lusts. Many are making merchandise of the souls of men and women. In Revelation it speaks of the fall of Babylon's merchants, and the last item in a list of many commodities is "souls of men" (Rev. 18:13). Then too, Jesus told of those who would say at the last day, "Lord, Lord, have we not prophesied in thy name? and in thy name have cast out devils? and in thy name done many wonderful works?" The Lord's startling response was, *"I never knew you: depart from me, ye that work iniquity"* (Matt. 7:22-23).

One of the outstanding things about the Book of Acts after the Day of Pentecost is that God could find men and women ready to leave what they were doing and go on His errands. He had hungry souls ready for harvest and He had men so mature and submissive that they took on the interests of the Lord and Master of the harvest field. "They followed the Lamb whithersoever He went."

Marvelous day when, having matured and lost all self-interest, we wish to repay in some small way His bounties bestowed upon us during our spiritual childhood, and we finally quiet ourselves in His presence, asking Him what is nearest His own great heart of love! How much more enriched we should be did we study His Word, allowing Him to speak to us regarding the wonderful, perfect, and acceptable will of God.

In these days, a volume of prayer is needed based on the entire Word of God. Often God permits our childish prayers to be answered, but with such consequences that we are brought to our knees as a humble suppliant, the wiser for having asked something contrary to the sayings of Jesus. Watch how you pray!

John Wesley taught his followers that they would have to hold success equally balanced by reproach. If great blessing—then great hatred, abuse, and scorning! John Wesley did not confine himself to a pulpit in order to reach the souls of men; already under much reproach, he was willing to make himself more vile in the eyes of the people by preaching in the fields and market place.

38

Robert Hall

Among the early Baptists in England we find men of prayer and great usefulness. One such was Robert Hall who enthralled his hearers though he may not have pleased all. The secret of his power with men was that he spent much time in solitude, for he who would take messages from the eternal God cannot be always in the presence of people lest his presentations be tarnished with worldly sentiments that mar the message of God coming clear through to his own soul.

Robert Hall's biographer says of his secret devotions: "Almost entirely without society, he spent much of his time in private devotions and not infrequently set apart whole days for prayer and fasting, a practice which he continued to the end of life, deeming it essential to the revival and preservation of personal religion. When able to walk he wandered in the fields and sought the shady grove, which often echoed with the voice of prayer, and witnessed the agony of his supplications. He was frequently so absorbed in these exercises as to be unaware of the approach of persons passing by, many of whom recollected with deep emotion the fervor and importunity of his addresses at the mercy seat, and the groaning which could not be uttered. His whole soul appears, indeed, to have been in a state of constant communion with God. His lonely walks amid the woodland scenery were rendered subservient to that end, and all his paths were bedewed with the tears of penitential prayer. Few men have spent more time in private devotion or resorted to it with more relish."

Anthony Norris Groves

The Brethren Movement took its rise both in England, and in Ireland. At that time, God wrought tremendously upon the hearts of not a few. Anthony Norris Groves, is not as well-known to the reading public as his brother-in-law, George Müller, but he was a very spiritual man, leaving a life-time impress upon George Müller. Reading his biography, *Anthony Norris Groves,* by G. H. Lang, we are impressed with the depth of spiritual life and clarity of understanding which are evident from his diary extracts and letters.

"How plainly we can see everywhere," he noticed, "that the absence of spiritual enjoyment of God, and finding all sufficiency in Him, is the real source of all declension: spiritual affections must be cultivated, for they grow not, so as to render their fruits to the careless husbandman;

warm and true affections toward God are indeed a spring of unmixed joy, yet how seldom with most are they in lively exercise."

"Wait on thy God continually," he wrote, "and the beginning of departure is found in only waiting upon God occasionally. There is something in the heart which tells us if we are really in fellowship with God; the soul that has tasted it cannot be mocked by an apparent return. One cause of going astray is the preferring something to God's worship even as Israel followed Baalim.

"Often we are beguiled into worldly things with an idea that we can make them subservient to God's glory; but the things we have thought would bend as a bow, to shoot arrows against the enemies of God, become the means of piercing us through with many sorrows, and leading us away from God. Nothing requires more spiritual discernment than to detect the snares of the enemy. They are often so covered over as to appear the leadings of God."

And finally a gem from his biographer: "Our strongest point needs perpetual guarding as much as our weakest, or, as the adage truly says, we fail at our strongest point. Moses had become the meekest of men, but Israel angered his spirit and he spake unadvisedly (Num. 20:10, Psa. 106:33). Groves had been a man of faith in communion with God beyond most, yet he suffered the outer life to overbalance the inner. Is not this a voice to tens of thousands of us, his brothers and sisters? A most devoted servant of God asked my thought as to taking up a further godly enterprise. I answered, 'Do it, if you are fully satisfied that you will have adequate time to pray over every detail of it continually.'"
(Used by permission of Paternoster Press, Exeter.)

G. H. Lang

Mr. Groves' biographer, G. H. Lang, was also noted for his prayer life. An author and traveling evangelist among the Brethren, he was a man of keen insight because he was a man of prayer and of the Word. Several small booklets written by him on prayer reveal the secrets shown to him over the years. At one time, he tells us in his autobiography, *An Ordered Life,* that he became concerned as to the fruitlessness of his ministry and besought God. He received his answer: "When I sought Him about this He answered: 'The apostles said, "We will give ourselves to prayer and the ministry of the word" (Acts 6:4). You have given yourself to the ministry of the word and to prayer: put these things in my order and I will work.' Forthwith I rearranged life to give one day a week to prayer, with a measure of fasting, and forthwith the Lord worked more powerfully. They that wait upon the mighty Jehovah change their human strength for His divine strength (Isa. 40:29-31). In the measure that this advances, they cease merely to tap at human hearts, but deliver sledge-hammer blows such as break the rock to pieces (Jer.23:29); they become strong enough to bind the strong and wicked spirits that bedarken and enslave souls, and so they can set their captives free (Luke 11:21,22)." (Used by permission of Paternoster Press, Exeter.)

Harold St. John

Harold St. John was another Brethren evangelist who traveled throughout the world leaving an influence that was outstanding. His daughter, Patricia St. John, is well known for her excellent books for children. She also wrote a biography of her father's life.

"How close we need to keep to God for such a holy ministry," he said, "and how soon the bloom wears off. Remember you're a polished shaft, but a breath can spoil the polish. Holy growth is subject to fixed laws, and I must obey them—much prayer, true Bible study, full self-control, right rein on thoughts. These are God's ways for me."

Another comment from him after a preaching session: "A bad day. Packed, over-flow meeting but all flat. I can't lecture on the Lord's coming. I don't live it enough. I was wrong in soul, away and out of touch. Got home heartily humiliated, though everybody else delighted with the service." We wonder how many modern evangelists would have come to the same conclusion after preaching to a packed audience accompanied by applause. God deepen the ministry today is our earnest prayer!

Some years ago we cut out a book review on Harold St. John from a magazine, but cannot discover who was the author. Part of this review we include here:

"Bible teachers used to bore me. Indeed, some of them still do! Their disputations about the meanings of remote words and theological trends seem to be so unrealistic and unrelated to life. But 'there was a man sent from God whose name was John'—St. John to be precise, but

41

pronounced Sinjun! God used him to transform my life in relation to Bible Study . . . he was a living exhibition of knowledge on fire. To me it is tragic that he wrote so little but a recently published biography (written by his daughter, the well-known Patricia St. John) preserves for us some (alas but a few!) of the precious nuggets he unearthed in his Bible Exploration.

"I used to marvel always at the way in which the Bible's text used to appear to pass continuously before his mind. We met together in the city of Manchester often enough for me to be amazed. Maybe I had been studying for some months a lesser known prophecy. He would say to me over lunch, 'Now, what have you been finding?' I would delve into intricacies beyond my grasp to which he would listen. Then, without so much as taking out his Bible, he would give a masterly review of the entire prophecy, quoting chapters and verses which I had good reason to know from months of study were accurate . . . but he had had no warning on the subject!! This happened so often that I can fully endorse Professor F. F. Bruce's statement, 'We younger men referred to him as "the maestro"' and Mr. Fred Mitchell, of the China Inland Mission, described him as 'the man who knew his Bible better than anyone else in Britain.'

"On one occasion the lights went out during a large meeting while he was reading an obscure passage, whereupon Mr. St. John went on quietly reciting the passage from memory. No wonder a lady said to him, 'I would give the world to know the Bible as you do.' 'Madam,' replied the young preacher with a courteous little bow, 'that is exactly what it cost.'"

A few quotations from his biography by his daughter will reveal to us the intimate communion this prayer warrior had with God through His Word:

"I need to help souls, not merely preach."

"A dispiriting lecture to a handful of resigned looking people."

"A full day, but lack of fullness of the Holy Spirit and confess it as sin."

"I must learn to speak only what I have really enjoyed with God."

"He has been through the fire," he said speaking of a well-known saint; "I have only looked at it."

"Before conversion the question is 'Heaven or hell?' Afterwards it becomes 'Heaven or earth?'"

"Do you build character of stone or brick? . . . Gen. 11:3, Isa. 9:10, Isa. 65:3 show how brick is man's little makeshift to avoid a crisis, but God uses stones—Living ones—see 1 Peter."

We return briefly to the book review for this final word: "The secret of having knowledge set on fire?—The Holy Spirit. . . . 'The Word,' he would say, 'The Word always—but never the Word without the Holy Spirit. . . . Beyond the sacred page I seek Thee, Lord, my Spirit yearns for Thee, Thou living Word!'

"Thus it was that the sunshine grew stronger until as a dying man he could whisper the question to a daughter, 'Did you ever see God?'

"'No, Daddy,' she answered.

"'I did,' came the labored reply, 'long, long ago. I've never told anyone about it but I'll tell you now when I've had a little rest' . . . but the secret was never revealed except the truth of it was evident to all, especially when, looking up radiantly awaiting the call, he expressed the ultimate of a lifetime of walking with God; "I am too weak to pray. I am too tired to love Him much, but I'm just lying here, letting Him love me.'"

> Why should we wonder at the flight
> Of any streaking satellite,
>   When every worshiping heart can share
>   A gold immensity of prayer
> That circles earth and reaches far
> Beyond the mightiest gleaming star—
>   More bright than any galaxy,
>   More wide than all infinity!
>   —Grace V. Watkins.
> (Used by Permission of *Herald of Holiness).*

Robert C. Chapman

The piety and godliness of Robert Chapman have few compeers. Although coming from a wealthy and cultured background, he sought to emulate the example of the Lord Jesus Christ, when he purchased a humble home near a tannery in a poor district in Barnstaple, Devon. Here this bachelor entertained the Lord's people as guests, and insisted on polishing their shoes. To one who complained that this was beneath his dignity, Chapman explained that we no longer wash the disciple's feet, and polishing their shoes was the nearest approach to this humble example of our Lord.

Signing away much of his wealth, he lived by faith, hoping thereby to stimulate the Lord's people to a life of simple trust for the necessaries of life. His own life was Spartan-like in its rigorous self-denial. "At four o'clock in the morning," his biographer, Frank Holmes, said, "he would be seen striding down the street and out of the town. These early morning walks sometimes took him to Ilfracombe for breakfast—twelve miles away over Devonshire hills. On one occasion, at least, he walked to Exeter—a distance of forty miles—before lunch. Normally, however, he would walk a few miles and then return to clean the shoes and call his guests.

"It will be gathered from this that he rarely rose later than 3:30 a.m. By his bedside was a large, square, lead-lined bath. Each night, punctually at 9 o'clock, he said 'Goodnight,' had a hot bath, and went to bed. Each morning, while the town was still asleep, he jumped into a cold bath, and then dressed. He once said to a visitor: 'You see, dear brother, God has given us a valuable body, and He expects us, as good workmen, to keep it in good order. I open the pores of my body at night and close them with a cold bath in the morning.'

"Up till midday, whether he was indoors or out, the greater part of his time was given up to prayer, Bible reading, and meditation. A conservative estimate would be seven hours of definite communion with God before noon. This was undoubtedly the secret of his spiritual power. The present generation of believers would do well to take heed to his example. Quietness and the strength that comes from long waiting on God are not always valued as they should be. The activity of the flesh is too often substituted for the power of the Spirit. A certain amount of work is rushed through. God is asked to bless what has been done, and plans are feverishly laid for the morrow.

"Robert Chapman got through a vast amount of work, but without a vast amount of stir and bustle. His life was like the steady flow of a mighty river, which is of far greater moment than the noisy trickle of a choked-up gutter.

"On Saturdays he gave his mind complete rest before the duties of the Lord's Day. He usually spent the whole day in his workshop. Walking and carpentry were his chief recreations, and Saturday was the day for carpentry. At the rear of his little cottage he had fitted up a tiny room for this purpose. Here there was a bench and a fine set of tools, but the main feature was a lathe. On it was turned innumerable bread boards. These he presented to his guests, or sold for missionary funds.

"Normally no one was permitted to see him on Saturdays. It was well understood by friends in the neighborhood that if they wanted to talk with him about some matter they should choose some other day. One highly favored young brother who ventured to the door of his workshop on one such occasion was told: 'You can come in. But talk about the lathe.'

"Yet even this recreation was accompanied by spiritual exercises, for he always fasted on Saturdays, and while he was working, poured out his soul in communion with his Lord. The habit of combining the spiritual and practical was characteristic of Chapman. He prayed as he walked or as he did household duties. In fact, he refused to recognize any artificial distinctions between religious and material duties, but was always conscious of the Divine command: 'Whatsoever ye do, do it heartily, as to the Lord, and not to men; knowing that of the Lord ye shall receive the reward of the inheritance; for ye serve the Lord Christ' (Col. 3:23-24).

"Perhaps in some ways Saturday was the richest day of the week for him; for on every other day his mind was occupied with pastoral matters. Saturday was a day given up to the necessary refreshment of his own mind and spirit. One who burst in upon him one Saturday in some emergency, said that his face shone as the face of an angel."

This patriarch was almost 100 years old when he went to be with His beloved Master, leaving behind him the fragrance of a life which had blessed that entire district in which he lived, moved, and had his being.

SCOTTISH PREACHERS

What a tremendous heritage the godly Scots of all generations have handed down to us! The secret is not difficult to find. It was not their rugged mountains that made them holy, for amongst their contemporaries were outlaws, profligates, and drunkards. It was surely not their naturally reserved nature that made them godly, or enabled them to send missionaries to the four corners of the globe out of all proportion to the sparse population of the land. Their secret was the same as that of any other godly people—they were men of prayer and great lovers of the Word of God. Their lives have shone down to us through succeeding generations because they were in touch with God through prayer. Let us, like them, learn to "Touch and Glow."

John Knox

Scottish Protestantism got off to a praying start. John Knox was a praying man first, and after that the national reformer and fiery preacher. "Give me Scotland or I die," was his vehement but reverent demand as he took his burden to the God he served so whole-heartedly. Little wonder that Mary Queen of Scots exclaimed that she feared the prayers of John Knox more than the armies of England. Poor woman! If only she had requested those prayers on her own behalf and had not run away from them, how different might have been the end of her story!

That era ushered in a host of praying men. The times demanded it. John Welch pleaded for Scotland for hours, walking up and down in the garden; or, wrapped in his tartan rug in his study, he would spend the night on his knees.

Samuel Rutherford

It was prayer that triumphantly conveyed those old Covenanters through the darkest but most glorious portion of their history. It was prayer that caused the saintly Rutherford to utter those words immortalized in hymnology, "Glory dwelleth in Emmanuel's land." So close was his communion with the Christ he loved, whether in his beloved "Dear Anwoth" or exiled in Aberdeen, that "Emmanuel's land" was never far away.

Samuel Rutherford's letters, written during his exile are unexcelled for their depth of spiritual content. Rutherford deplored the sin and irregularities of which he had been guilty in his early youth, and sought to help others to see the necessity of true repentance. He was deprived of his wife and two children when death took them from him, but he still took comfort in his parishioners and their spiritual needs. He learned through his sufferings that the soul thrives best in the winter of affliction.

Such depth of truth as this man shared with his correspondents was not gained by a casual visit to the Throne of Grace. Before dawn of day, this saintly Scotsman was up seeking the face of the Savior Whom he came to so passionately love. His losses brought infinite gain to the Body of Christ, for had he not been denied the pulpit and been consequently confined, we should have been robbed of his excellent letters written to his friends of the Covenant.

Alexander Peden

It was prayer that made a cave a Bethel to "Auld Sandy" Peden as he would hide from the troopers and prepare his message for his next secret Conventicle up some secluded glen. And, oh, how naturally he prayed when in dire peril! Once, while standing on a prominent point preaching, his enemies' coming was suddenly announced. Then how simply did he ask the God he knew so well to put down His cloak and "cover puir Auld Sandy." Heaven spontaneously answered and down came the inimitable "Scotch Mist" under the cover of which he once more could make his escape.

John Livingstone

How inspiring are those landmarks of revival—the "Preaching Braes" of Cambuslang of Whitefield memory; Dundee and Kilsyth where the praying William Burns was so blessed! And then there is the "Kirk o' Shotts." Alexander Whyte, in his book, *Samuel Rutherford and Some of his Correspondents,* tells us about the all-night of prayer at Shotts which preceded the mighty outpouring of God upon a large

47

audience, resulting in the conversion of 500 persons. We had never realized, however, that the revival was, to quote one report, "more due to Lady Culross than to any other human being. True, John Livingstone preached the Thanksgiving Sermon, but it was through Lady Culross's influence that he was got to preach it. He preached it after a night of prayer spent by Lady Culross and her companions, so that we read of next day's sermon and its success as a matter of course.

"I cannot venture to tell a heterogeneous audience the history of that night they spent at Shotts with God. It is so unlike what we have ever seen or heard of. There may be one or two of us here who have spent whole nights in prayer at some crisis in our life, going from one promise to another, when, in the Psalmist's words, the sorrows of death compassed us, and the pains of hell gat hold upon us. And we, one or two of us, may have had miracles from Heaven forthwith performed upon us, fit to match in a private way with the hand of God on the Kirk of Shotts. But even those of us who have such secrets between us and God, we, I fear, never spent a whole Communion night, never shutting our eyes but to pray for a baptism of spiritual blessing upon tomorrow's congregation. What a mother in Israel was Lady Culross, with five hundred children born of her travail in one day."

Writing later to Livingstone, who was undergoing persecution, Lady Culross did not promise wealth, health, and happiness. She wrote: "You must be hewn and hammered and drest and prepared before you can be a *Leiving-Ston* fit for His building. And if He is minded to make you meet to help others, you must look for another manner of strokes than you have yet felt. . . . But when you are laid low, and are vile in your own eyes, then He will raise you up and refresh you with some blinks of His favorable countenance, that you may be able to comfort others with those consolations wherewith you have been comforted of Him . . . . Since God has put His work in your weak hands, look not for long ease here. You must feel the full weight of your calling; a weak man with a strong God. The pain is but a moment, the pleasure is everlasting. . . . Cross upon cross; the end of one with me is but the beginning of another."

Alexander Whyte

Alexander Whyte was yet another very godly Scotsman of unusual insight. His utter hatred of sin and hypocrisy, his love for secret prayer, and his most serious outlook upon the entire Christian walk—all may be discovered in his writings which he has left us as his legacy that we might benefit thereby.

Blessed with a courageous mother of some force of character, Alexander was born out of wedlock, but his mother refused to marry the father of the lad. Whether she had such a profound sense of her sin or not, we do not know, but she consequently turned down several offers of marriage, disdaining to hand her charge over to any other for his life training. She must have braved the innuendoes of neighbors whose lives may not have been as faultless as her own in the eyes of the Righteous Judge. This may account for the intense hatred for sin which this astute preacher revealed in his writings and sermons.

But let us look into the prayer life of this greatly used Scottish minister. A member of his congregation once came to him after his sermon saying, "It went to my heart as if you had come straight from the Audience Chamber."

"And perhaps I did," he solemnly replied.

"Pray after the sermon. . . . Prayer for ourselves and the people after preaching is much neglected. Do not neglect either," advised Whyte.

"With his closet, and with the key of his closet continually in his hand, no minister need despair, even though he is not a great orator with a great gift of public prayer."

"'Apart! Apart!' This great prophet keeps ringing in every minister's ears. Every minister—of all men—apart!" wrote Barbour, Whyte's biographer.

"Much as he valued the privilege of public worship," continues Barbour, "carefully as he prepared his own share in it—yet to him the typical and the highest form of devotion was secret prayer. This came out in his startling reply to the question of a young minister whether he advised the preparation of prayers for the pulpit: 'Certainly I do; but public prayer is an unnatural act.' The same thought is developed in the sermon on 'The Secret Burden,' based on one of his favorite passages in the prophets—that in Zechariah, in which the word 'apart' occurs eleven times in three verses. Discipline, Prayer, the Interior Motive, Humility before God and men, Purity attained through Suffering—these were among the master-notes of his preaching."

"If you pray much apart, you are already beyond your depth. You are wiser than all your teachers."

Prayer was to him a most serious business, and he warned others that it was no picnic to spend hours prevailing with God.

"You must understand that prayer, to be called prayer, is not what you hear people all about you calling prayer. That is not prayer. Jacob's thigh was out of joint, and our Lord's sweat was as it were great drops of blood falling to the ground. Prayer is colossal work. There were giants in those days. Prayer takes all our heart, and all our soul, and all our strength, and all our mind, and all our life, sleeping and waking. Prayer is the priceliest, the noblest, the most unearthly act on this side of Heaven. Only pray, then; only pray aright, and enough, and it will change your whole nature as it changed Jacob's. Till, from the meanest, the falsest, the most treacherous, the most deceitful, the most found-out, and the most miserable of men, it will make you also a very prince with God and with men. Happy is he that hath the God of Jacob for his help!"

"Jacob had twenty years, and more, of sin and of sorrow, of remorse and of repentance, of gratitude for such a miraculous past, and of beaten-back effort after a better life, and then, to crown all, he had that unparalleled night of fear and prayer at the Jabbok; a night's work such that even the Bible has nothing else like it till our Lord's night in Gethsemane."

In his book, *Lord, Teach us to Pray,* Whyte mentions the praying of James: "James, the brother of the Lord, and the author of this Epistle, was nicknamed 'Camel-knees' by the early Church. James had been so slow of heart to believe that his brother, Jesus, could possibly be the Christ, that, after he was brought to believe, he was never off his knees. And when they came to coffin him, it was like coffining the knees of a camel rather than the knees of a man, so hard, so worn, so stiff were they with prayer, and so unlike any other dead man's knees they had every coffined."

Whyte beautifully expresses our duty to pray for our friends: "Our friends! How bad we all are to our friends! How short-sighted, how cruel, how thoughtless, how inconsiderate! We send them gifts. Our children cover their Christmas tree with Christmas presents to our friends. Our friends cost us a great deal of thought and trouble and money, from time to time. We send them sheaves of cards with all manner of affectionate devices and verses. We take time and we write our old friends, at home and abroad, letters full of news and of affection on Christmas Day and on New Year's Day. But we never pray for them! Or, at best, we pray for them in a great hurry.

"Why do we do everything for our friends, but the best thing? How few of us shut our door during all the leisure of the last two weeks, and deliberately, and particularly, and with discrimination, and with importunity prayed for our dearest and best friends! We discriminate in our purchases for our friends, lest we should slight or offend our friends; but not in our prayers.

"Who in the family, who in the congregation, who in the city, who abroad, will be surprised by some blessing this year? Surprised—with some unexpected providence, some despaired-of deliverance, some cross lifted off, or left and richly blessed, some thorn taken out of their flesh, some salvation they had not themselves had faith to ask for? And all because we asked, and importuned, and 'shut our door' upon God and ourselves in their behalf. A friend of any kind, and to any extent and degree, is something to have in this cold and lonely world. But to have a friend who has the ear of God and who fills God's ear from time to time with our name and our case—Oh, where shall I find such a friend? Oh, who shall find such a friend henceforth in me?"

"God's goodness
Came to me just now on a friend's prayer.
I clearly knew them both.
Strange!
A prayer (that priceless gift); given me,
Arrives, laden with God.

"Are prayers, I wonder,
Empty dishes we present to God
For conveyance of His great goodness?
Why, then, aren't more prayers given?
Why are we stingy with a prayer,
When we need prayer so much ourselves?"
                                    —By Marguerite Estaver.
(Used by permission as published in the *Wesleyan Methodist*).

51

Dr. Whyte formulated an excellent rule for public prayer to which every Christian ought to adhere. "It would be an ostentation and a presumption to pray for other men in public, as you are permitted and enabled and commanded to pray for them in private. It would be resented, and never forgiven. In intercessory prayer in public, particulars and instances, and actual persons, and special and peculiar cases, are absolutely impracticable and impossible. You simply dare not pray, in public, for other men—any more than for yourself—as they need to be prayed for. You would be arrested and imprisoned under the law of libel if you did it. Were you to see these men and women around you as they are; and were you to describe them, and to plead with God to redeem and renew, and restore, and save them—the judge would shut your mouth.

"But in private, neither your friend nor your enemy will ever know, or even guess, till the last day, what they owe to you, and to your closet. You will never incur either blame or resentment or retaliation by the way you speak about them and their needs in the ear of God. The things that are notoriously and irrevocably destroying the character and the usefulness of your fellow-worshiper—you may not so much as whisper them to your best friend, or to his. But you can, and you must, bear him by name, and all his sins and vices, all that is deplorable, and all that is contemptible about him, before God. And if you do so; and if you persist and persevere in doing so—though you would not believe it—you will come out of your closet to love, and to honor, and to put up with, and to protect, and to defend your client the more—the more you see what is wrong with him, and the more you importune God in his behalf."

MORE SCOTTISH PREACHERS

Robert Murray McCheyne

The name of Robert Murray McCheyne, the well-known Scottish saint, became almost a household word as a result of the very well-read biography of his life by Andrew Bonar, his contemporary and intimate friend and associate. Born in Edinburgh, May 21, 1813, McCheyne, from a child, was of a poetic and musical turn of mind, and very susceptible to spiritual influences. He was fond of his worldly pleasures however, until the death of his older brother, David, brought him abruptly to think of eternity and the brevity of time.

Conviction continued to deepen, making him to know the depths of his inward pollution and causing his worldly pleasures to pall upon him. Diary entries read something like this: "I hope never to play cards again." "Never visit on a Sunday evening again." "Absented myself from the dance, upbraidings ill to bear. But I must try to bear the cross."

At twenty-three years of age he was ordained and then was inducted into the church of St. Peter's at Dundee. Here was a large parish of 4,000 people, many of whom never darkened a church door. His members numbered 1,100, and the young minister set himself to earnestly labor for their salvation, saying, "He has set me down among the noisy mechanics and political weavers of this godless town. . . . Perhaps the Lord will make this wilderness of chimney-tops to be green and beautiful as the garden of the Lord, a field which the Lord hath blessed." He met on Saturdays with Andrew Bonar of a neighboring town, as well as with several other earnest young ministers, to pray for one another, and especially for blessing on the Sabbath.

It was not long before he had instituted the Thursday night prayer-meeting for his people, for he had read how united prayer in a church had brought blessing to an entire district. Here he would give out a verse, pray both before and after, announce the outline of his text, and then read to them some history of revivals making a few comments. "A number of people come from all parts of the town," he wrote to his friend, Andrew Bonar. "But oh! I need much the living Spirit to my own soul; I want my life to be hid with Christ in God. At present there is too much hurry and bustle and outward working to allow the calm working of the Spirit on the heart. I seldom get time to meditate, like Isaac, at even-tide, except when I am tired; but the dew comes down when all nature is at rest—when every leaf is still."

His very presence wrought strangely upon his congregation. As one old man noted, "Before he opened his lips, as he came along the passage, there was something about him that sorely affected me." McCheyne desired, in his method of delivery, to go back to the primitive days of the Christian Church. Someone once asked him if he was not afraid he would run short of sermons, and he replied, "No, I am just an interpreter of Scripture in my sermons; and when the Bible runs dry, then I shall." He had a wholesome fear of grieving the Holy Spirit and desired to "preach the mind of the Spirit in a passage," endeavoring to present Christ in every sermon. He spoke of himself as "strong as a giant when in the Church, but a willow-wand when all was over."

At a prayer meeting for young men he once counseled, "Remember the most spiritual prayer is a 'groan which cannot be uttered.'" The godly, however, are never held in repute as Jesus warned. "If ye were of the world, the world would love his own: but because ye are not of the world, but I have chosen you out of the world, therefore the world hateth you." His biographer said, "He had much reproach to bear. He was the object of supercilious contempt to formal, cold-hearted ministers, and of bitter hatred to many of the ungodly. . . . Very deep was the enmity borne to him by some—all the deeper, because the only cause of it was his likeness to his Master. But nothing turned him aside."

His diary records are very inspiring and will speak to those of us who are too often prodded into outward activities rather than secret communing.

"Two things that defile this day in looking back are love of praise running through all and consenting to listen to worldly talk at all. Oh that these may keep me humble and be my burden, leading me to the cross. Then, Satan, thou wilt be outwitted."

"When I was laid aside from the ministry, I used often to say, 'Now God is teaching me the use of prayer.' I thought I would never forget the lesson, yet I fear I have grown slack again when in the midst of my work."

"Private meditation exchanged for conversation. Here is the root of all evil—forsake God, and He forsakes us."

"Sabbath—very happy in my work. Too little prayer in the morning. Must try to get early to bed on Saturday, that I may 'rise a great while before day.'"

"Rose early to seek God, and found Him Whom my soul loveth. Who would not rise early to meet such company?"

In letters to his correspondents, he often extolled prayer. "King Jesus is a good Master. I have had some sweet seasons of communion with an unseen God which I would not give up for thousands of gold and silver. May you have much of His presence with you!"

"Are there not some spots," he wrote to a friend, "that you can call Peniel, where you have met Jehovah-Jesus face to face? When you do get into His presence, oh do not weary of it; do not soon let go your hold."

"I trust that you are keeping strong, and able to enjoy the open air, and that your souls all prosper, that you have often such times as Jacob had at Mahanaim, when the angels of God met him, or such times as that at Peniel, when God had to cry out. 'Let me go, for the day breaketh.'"

Andrew Bonar said that it was only a few months before his death that he drew up considerations touching "Reformation in Secret Prayer." "I ought," said McCheyne, "to spend the best hours of the day in communion with God. It is my noblest and most fruitful employment, and is not to be thrust into any corner."

Andrew Bonar

Andrew Bonar, beloved minister and pastor, was a great admirer of McCheyne and he, too, was eminent for his prayer life. He and his hymn-writer brother, Horatius, had a precious heritage in a praying father and mother. Bonar's writings breathe out aspirations for personal communion with God on a deep level and also constantly urge us all to pray more effectively. We pass on these pungent out-breathings:

"More carefully than ever I hope this year to give two hours before going out every day to meditation on the Word and prayer."

"I see that I will need every day more and more in the morning, before any business begins, a cup of the new wine of the kingdom—fellowship with God."

"Rose a little earlier than usual to fast and pray. I see that fasting and retirement, along with prayer, should go together. The effect upon the body and soul is somewhat like affliction. It brings down the tone of the spirit, subdues the flesh, draws off the soul from self-complacency, and makes the flesh unsatisfying. It discovers much to me that is humbling; it helps to remove my lightness of mind."

"I ought to put into practice in common duties that saying: 'Seek ye first the kingdom of God.' By the grace of God and the strength of His Holy Spirit I desire to lay down the rule not to speak to man until I have spoken with God; not to do anything with my hand till I have been upon my knees; not to read letters or papers until I have read something of the Holy Scriptures. I hope also to be able at 'cool of day' to pray and meditate upon the name of the Lord. It may be an Eden here."

"Last night, in reviewing the past time, nothing shamed me more than the sin of praying little, when we might ask in Christ's name so much, and receive so much. We have stood at the well all day, and scarce drawn up a few drops. Only this I feel, that if I have not drunk much of the Fountain of living waters, I have not, on the other hand, filled the place by broken cisterns; for hours without God have been to me hours of no delight and no strength."

"Time of prayer alone and in expectation of meeting some of the brethren at mid-day. I feel exceedingly how little I really converse with God. My prayer is like a calling to one distant, not unbosoming myself to one beside me."

"May we so enjoy communion with Thee that when we lose it we may feel just as if we were away from our home."

Bonar practiced what he preached. His whole life was one which was organized and disciplined to pray. The more he prayed, the more he felt the need of praying. Entry after entry shows the determined and persistent struggle to be a deep man of prayer.

"In prayer in the wood for some time, having set apart three hours of devotion: felt drawn out much to pray for that peculiar fragrance which believers have about them, who are much in fellowship with God. . . . Yesterday got a day to myself for prayer. With me every time of prayer, or almost every time, begins with a conflict. It is my deepest regret that I pray so little. I could count the days, not by what I have of new instances of usefulness, but by the times I have been enabled to pray in faith, and to take hold upon God.

"I see that unless I keep up short prayer every day throughout the whole day, at intervals, I lose the spirit of prayer. . . . Too much work without corresponding prayer. Today setting myself to pray. The Lord forthwith seems to send a dew upon my soul . . . . Passed six hours today in prayer and Scripture-reading, confessing sin, and seeking blessing for myself and the parish.

"For nearly ten days past have been much hindered in prayer, and feel my strength weakened thereby. I must at once return, through the Lord's strength, to not less than three hours a day spent in prayer and meditation upon the Word.

"Tomorrow I propose to spend the most of the day in prayer in the Church. Lord, help me."

Later, we find him setting apart one whole day in each month for prayer and fasting. But his devotion overflowed all prepared channels. Sentences such as these carry with them their own instruction:

"Felt in the evening most bitter grief over the apathy of the district. They are perishing! They are perishing! And yet they will not consider. I lay awake, thinking over it, and crying to the Lord in broken groans."

"Workers cannot begin their work without a passage of Scripture for themselves. William Burns, when asked on one occasion to speak, said, 'No, I have not yet got a morsel for myself.' Try to act upon this principle, and remember it must be fresh manna, just gathered. I should feel ashamed to take withered flowers to the sick."

"Have been enabled during the week to pray every day for help by setting apart an hour in addition for this end; the benefit appeared today in a remarkable liberty in speaking to my flock about the past twelve years."

At the Perth Conference: "Much exercised about getting power from on high, about which much conversation. I am rather disappointed that there is not more prayer throughout the day, but the atmosphere is delightful, so much brotherly love, so much Biblical truth, so much delight in whatever exalts Christ."

"Prayer is seed sown on the heart of God."

"Prayer will be very lame and dry if it does not come from reading the Scriptures."

I tell Him all my sorrows,
I tell Him all my joys;
I tell Him all that pleases me,
I tell Him what annoys;
He tells me what I ought to do,
He tells me what to try,
And so we walk together,
My Lord and I.
　　　　　　—Mrs. Shorey.

John Brown

"I would not exchange the learning of one hour's fellowship with Christ for all the liberal learning in ten thousand universities during ten thousand years, even though angels were to be my teachers," said John Brown. Was it because he belittled human learning? Not in the slightest, for a more ardent student one could scarcely find. He studied into the small hours of the morning, allowing himself very little time for sleep, thus undermining a strong constitution. He was proficient in Latin, Greek, and Hebrew, which he had begun to learn when only an orphan lad tending sheep for a neighboring farmer. He also acquired understanding in another eight languages, besides his stores of knowledge in history and theology.

The cynic and critic David Hume listened to John Brown preach and said later, "That's the man for me. He means what he says. He speaks as if Jesus was at his elbow." And Hume was not far wrong, for the Lord was always near to him as he assiduously gave himself to prayer and the ministry as had the early disciples in the Book of Acts. He rose in summer at four or five o'clock and continued until eight at night with only intermission for meals and family worship twice daily.

This godly Scotsman preached five sermons each Sabbath. They were of one hour each, and were memorized often in the spirit of prayer so that his warm heart feelings would impregnate the message. His biographer said, "Such was his acquaintance with the Scriptures of truth that if a text were mentioned, he could not only repeat it accurately, but trace its connection and give the sense. He contributed to the book world 29 different publications, notable among these his *Dictionary of the Bible* which was widely used at the time.

We are indebted to Scotland for giving to the religious world such apostolic ministers and missionaries, for they had much to do with deepening the ideals of the Gospel in their day and age.

Lachlan MacKenzie

Lachlan MacKenzie, a Highland preacher, possessed remarkable gifts of discernment. His biographer states, "It is recorded of him that he had stated that he never brought the cause of a sinner before the Mercy Seat but the Lord revealed to him the sinner's condition and what he was to do with him."

Again we may look at the habitual conduct of his life for his secret: "His prayerfulness was the leading feature of his Christianity. . . . Much of his time was spent on his knees, and many a sleepless night he passed, sometimes wrestling, as for his life, against the assaults of the tempter and at other times rejoicing in the hope of the glory of God. The nearness to the Mercy Seat to which he was sometimes admitted was quite extraordinary. Proof of this might be given, because of which we cannot wonder that he had the fame and the influence of a prophet among the simple people of the North, although the record of the proof would cause much incredulous nodding of the wise heads of the South. Avoiding the extreme of a superstitious credulity on the one hand, and of the formalist's skepticism on the other, it is altogether safe to say that Mr. Lachlan MacKenzie enjoyed peculiar intercourse with God, and received such distinct intimations of His mind, in reference to the cases which he carried to the Mercy Seat, as but very few of God's children have obtained."

Monod

"Lord, teach me to pray! Ah! if I were to return to life, I would with the help of God and in distrust of myself, give much more time to prayer than I have hitherto done, reckoning much more upon the effect of that than on my own labors; which, however, it is our duty never to neglect, but which has no strength but in so far as it is animated by prayer."

"It is by prayer that we maintain that communion with Jesus Christ which will render us capable of doing what He did, and being what He was: but it is by the prayer of faith—persevering, ardent prayer, which takes no refusal, but will enjoy all that the Father has promised in His Word, and will not be silent—by prayer upon our knees, which wrestles on through blood and tears till it has obtained what it asked.

"More ships!" some cry; "more guns!"
   "More fighters in the air!"
But, wise the king who adds,
   "More prayer!"

Remember, angels use
   This ancient thoroughfare;
So keep their highway clear—
   More prayer!

One day will not suffice
   To meet time's wear and tear,
Each hour of life must see
   More prayer!

Again and yet again,
   The scrolls of God declare:
"The deepest need of men—
   More prayer!"
                 —Unknown.

WELSH PREACHERS

"Oh, for five hundred Elijahs," exclaimed Charles Spurgeon, "each one upon his Carmel, crying unto God, and we should soon have the clouds bursting into showers! Oh, for more prayer, more constant, incessant prayer! Then the blessing would rain upon us."

Truly if those who ministered unto us came from the secret place of prayer, having prevailed with God, our services would more often witness the mighty power of God released. Our converts would bear the impress of that deepening type of preaching. Let us bear out this conviction by a few examples of Welsh preachers who had felt their own insufficiency and so received a fresh enduement of power. Wales, in days gone by, had her Elijahs praying through before entering the pulpit.

Christmas Evans

Trials sore were pressing in upon the Welsh preacher, Christmas Evans. To have hanging over him the threat of a law suit was extremely distressing to this saintly man. It would have been bad enough if extravagant living on his part had occasioned this debt, but he had barely enough to live on and only he and his godly partner knew the kind of houses they had lived in for the Gospel's sake.

No! It was the debt that Christmas Evans had incurred through building chapels in areas of Wales where there was no meeting house which so weighed upon him. As the crowds had increased as a result of God's blessing on the indefatigable labors of this praying preacher, the urgent need for meeting houses had arisen. Then, too, the conference would sometimes send this humble man to places where the debt upon the building had not previously been met. Now, the threat of legal procedure seemed imminent.

"They talk," he said, "of casting me into a court of law, where I have never been, and I hope I shall never go; but I will cast them, first, into the court of Jesus Christ."

61

Christmas Evans was in the habit of putting on paper his prayers and communions with God. "I knew there was no ground of action," he continued, "but, still, I was much disturbed, being, at the time, sixty years of age, and having, very recently, buried my wife. . . . I received the letter at a monthly meeting at one of the contests with spiritual wickedness in high places. On my return home, I had fellowship with God, during the whole journey of ten miles, and, arriving at my own house, I went upstairs to my own chamber, and poured forth my heart before the Redeemer, Who has in His hands all authority and power."

We record the prayer for it would seem to be a petition which was prompted by the Holy Spirit. The Bible says that we do not know how to pray as we ought, but that the Great Teacher, the Holy Spirit, would teach us how to pray and would pray in us. It is this kind of prayer that receives an answer because the Spirit knows what is the mind of God.

"O blessed Lord! In Thy merit, I confide, and trust to be heard. Lord, some of my brethren have run wild; and forgetting their duty, and obligations to their father in the Gospel, they threaten me with the law of the land. Weaken, I beseech Thee, their designs in this, as Thou didst wither the arm of Jeroboam; and soften them, as Thou didst soften the mind of Esau and disarmed him of his warlike temper against Thy servant Jacob, after the wrestling at Penuel. So disarm them, for I do not know the length of Satan's chain in this case, and in this unbrotherly attack. But Thou canst shorten the chain as short as it may please Thee.

"Lord, I anticipate them in point of law. They think of casting Thine unworthy servant into the little courts here below; but I cast my cause into the High Court, in which Thou, gracious Jesus, art the High Chancellor. Receive Thou the cause of Thine unworthy servant, and send him a writ, or a notice, immediately—sending into their conscience, and summoning them to consider what they are doing. Oh, frighten them with a summons from Thy court, until they come, and bow in contrition at Thy feet; and take from their hands every revengeful weapon, and make them deliver up every gun of scandal, and every sword of bitter words, and every spear of slanderous expressions and surrender them all at Thy cross.

"Forgive them all their faults, and clothe them with white robes, and give them oil for their heads, and the organ, and the harp of ten strings, to sing, for the trampling of Satan under our feet by the God of peace."

"I went up once," he says, "and was about ten minutes in prayer; I felt some confidence that Jesus heard. I went up again with a tender heart; I could not refrain from weeping with the joy of hope that the Lord was drawing near to me. After the seventh struggle I came down, fully believing that the Redeemer had taken my cause into His hands, and that He would arrange, and manage for me.

"My countenance was cheerful, as I came down the last time, like Naaman, having washed himself seven times in the Jordan; or Bunyan's Pilgrim, having cast his burden at the foot of the cross, in the grave of Jesus. I well remember the place—the little house adjoining the meeting house, at Dildwrn, where I then resided—in which this struggle took place. I can call it Penuel. No weapon intended against me prospered, and I had peace at once to my mind, and in my (temporal) condition. I have frequently prayed for those who would injure me, that they might be blessed, even as I have been blessed. I know not what would have become of me, had it not been for those furnaces in which I have been tried, and in which the spirit of prayer has been excited, and exercised in me."

The threat was never carried out, and the intercessor heard no more about it. He had laid his case upon the desk of the Judge of all the earth in that prayer. But trouble did not cease to dog the footsteps of that saintly man of God. His biographer tells us: "Indeed, clouds of trouble were thickening around him. It often seems that trouble, in the ministerial life, comes exactly at that moment when the life is least able to stand, with strength, against it; and, certainly, in the life of Christmas Evans, sorrows gathered and multiplied at the close."

There is nothing that can so dull the spiritual edge of one's experience as getting into controversy. Heresy is one of the works of the flesh, and in any church, at any time, this is one of the evils which will confront the laborers for God.

This form of trouble Christmas Evans encountered earlier in his ministry when a controversy arose among the Baptist societies and almost engulfed them. John Richard Jones was the leader of what was called the Sandemanian heresy, and he was a brilliant man, claiming to have adopted some of the primitive practices of the early Church. He separated himself from others and severely criticized those who would not completely disassociate themselves from individuals who did not follow the same teaching. Christmas Evans agreed with some aspects of the controversy, but in his zeal to refute the evil, gave way to ill-feeling and bitterness which arrested the spirit of prayer and life in his soul. No one save those who experience it know the depth of sorrow that follows when the Lord hides His face, and the upspringing well of water in the innermost being has been temporarily stopped. Prayer brought about his renewal.

"I was weary of a cold heart towards Christ and His sacrifice and the work of His Spirit—of a cold heart in the pulpit, in secret prayer and in the study. For fifteen years previously, I had felt my heart burning within, as if going to Emmaus with Jesus.

"On a day ever to be remembered by me, as I was going from Dolgelly to Machynlleth and climbing up towards Cader Idris, I considered it to be incumbent upon me to pray, however hard I felt in my heart, and however worldly the frame of my spirit was. Having begun in the name of Jesus, I soon felt, as it were, the fetters loosening, and the old hardness of heart softening, and, as I thought, mountains of frost and snow dissolving and melting within me.

"This engendered confidence in my soul in the promise of the Holy Ghost. I felt my whole mind relieved from some great bondage. Tears flowed copiously, and I was constrained to cry out for the gracious visits of God, by restoring to my soul the joys of His salvation; and that He would visit the churches in Anglesey that were under my care. I embraced in my supplications all the churches of the saints and nearly all the ministers in the Principality by their names.

"This struggle lasted for three hours; it rose again and again, like one wave after another, or a high flowing tide, driven by a strong wind, until my nature became faint by weeping and crying. Thus I resigned myself to Christ, body and soul, gifts and labors—all my life—every day, and every hour that remained for me; and all my cares I committed to Christ. The road was mountainous and lonely, and I was wholly alone and suffered no interruption in my wrestlings with God.

"From this time, I was made to expect the goodness of God, to churches and to myself. Thus the Lord delivered me, and the people of Anglesey from being carried away by the flood of Sandemanianism. In the first religious meetings after this, I felt as if I had been removed from the cold and sterile regions of spiritual frost, into the verdant fields of divine promises. The former striving with God in prayer and that longing anxiety for the conversions of sinners which I had experienced at Lleyn were now restored. I had a hold of the promises of God. The result was when I returned home, the first thing that arrested my attention was that the Spirit was working also in the brethren in Anglesey, inducing in them a spirit of prayer."

Rev. Griffith

There is a touching incident told of the Rev. Griffith of Caernarvon, who was to preach one night in a farm house. Some hours before the service was to begin, he asked for a retired spot in which to prepare for the evening service. The congregation had already assembled, but there was no sign of the minister. A servant in the family was sent to his room to request him to come as the people had been waiting for some time.

On approaching the door of his room, she heard what she supposed to be a dialogue carried on in a subdued tone of voice. Listening before knocking, she heard one say to the other, "I will not go unless Thou come with me."

The girl returned to the master of the house and told him that Rev. Griffiths had someone in the room with him, and that he would not come unless the other accompany him. "I did not hear the other reply, so I conclude he will not come from there tonight."

"Yes, I am sure he will come," replied the master of the house, "and the Other will come with him. We shall begin the service by singing and reading till the two come."

At last the minister made his appearance, and it was evident that Someone else came with him for it was no ordinary service they had that night. It was but the beginning of a powerful revival in the neighborhood where many were born of God.

Rees Howells

In the year 1879, two outstanding Welshmen were born not many miles apart who were to have astounding effects upon not only Wales, but the world. One was Evan Roberts, and the other was Rees Howells. Both were men of prayer and the Word. One was to influence the world in a brief display of God's power at the beginning of the century; the influence of the other, Rees Howells, was to be spread over a much longer period in which the intercessor was being thoroughly trained for wide-spread ministry to the world.

In Norman Grubb's book, *Rees Howells, Intercessor,* the reader cannot fail to receive blessing and instruction in that magnificent but almost lost art of intercession. Here was a man who would give himself up to months of intensive prayer just for one individual until he had received an answer. Passing from prayer for one person, he gradually attained the position of interceding for the nations of the world, and for the magnificent band of full-time missionaries at work all over the globe.

The one thing that appeals to us is the fact that he depended upon the Holy Spirit to guide his praying. He heard often from the Lord as to the next subject for his prayer concern. It was no unusual thing for Rees Howells to know the Lord's mind on the individual he was praying for, and this gave him an authority in prayer as well as physical strength to go through self-denials in food and sleep. He felt that he must enter into the life of the one for whom he prayed. This meant that he sacrificed lovely home-cooked meals prepared by his mother for bread and cheese when praying for a drunkard. He experienced "being continually delivered unto death" as he yielded physical life and reputation in order to pray through.

After giving himself to six months of intercession for a certain man, he went back to normal life, but the call came again to re-enter the hidden ministry for child widows in India. He gave himself for this purpose for four months. In order to ally himself with their condition, he gave up bread, tea, and sugar, and ate one meal of porridge every two days. In order not to distress his mother, he left home and lived in rooms. "He began the day at 5 a.m., with no food all day, then sleeping on the floor, up again at 5 o'clock and going another day without food until 5 p.m."

"'What pangs of hunger I had,' he said afterwards. 'The Lord doesn't make it easy for you. He doesn't carry you through on eagle's wings, as it were. The victory is that you come up through it. I remember the feeling I had the first day, when I had no bread at all. I would have given anything for a crust. When you take the place of another, you take the suffering of another; you have to walk every inch of it. As every meal-time came round, there was nothing for me. The wonder is that I didn't go under to it and give in. Only Ezekiel was my friend, and all I could say was, "How did he do it?"'" (Ezek. 4).

It must not be thought that intercession for Mr. Howells merely meant costly acts of obedience. With his own pangs, there went up a continual cry to God for the relief of the sufferers whose burden he was carrying.

When considering founding the Bible College in Swansea, South Wales, he went aside for ten months, praying from 6 a.m. to 5 p.m., at which time he took one meal. Can we wonder that such a man was led to make decisions which affected the lives of thousands?

A few words from his biographer on the subject of intercessory prayer might be of immense benefit to the readers of this book. Samuel Rees Howells, his son, who has undertaken to carry on the work his father so ably presided over, is likewise an intercessor, and he kindly gave permission for us to use extracts from his father's biography:

"That God seeks intercessors, but seldom finds them, is plain from the pain of His exclamation through Isaiah, 'He saw that there was no man, and wondered that there was no intercessor'; and His protest of disappointment through Ezekiel: 'I sought for a man among them that should make up the hedge, and stand in the gap before Me for the land . . . but I found none.'

"Perhaps believers in general have regarded intercession as just some form of rather intensified prayer. It is, so long as there is great emphasis on the word 'intensified;' for there are three things to be seen in an intercessor, which are not necessarily found in ordinary prayer: **identification, agony, and authority.**

"The identification of the intercessor with the ones for whom he intercedes is perfectly seen in the Savior. Of Him it was said that 'He poured out His soul unto death; and He was numbered with the transgressors, and He bare the sin of many, and made intercession for the transgressors. . . .' By taking our nature upon Himself, by learning obedience through the things which He suffered, by being tempted in all points like as we are, by becoming poor for our sakes, and finally by being made sin for us, He gained the position in which, with the fullest authority as the captain of our salvation made perfect through sufferings, and the fullest understanding of all we go through, He can ever live to make intercession for us, and by effective pleadings with the Father 'is able to save to the uttermost them that come unto God by Him.' Identification is thus the first law of the intercessor. He pleads effectively because he gives his life for those he pleads for; he is their genuine representative; he has submerged his self-interest in their needs and sufferings, and as far as possible has literally taken their place.

"There is another Intercessor, and in Him we see the agony of this ministry; for He, the Holy Spirit, 'maketh intercession for us with groanings which cannot be uttered.' This One, the only present Intercessor on earth, has no hearts upon which He can lay His burdens and no bodies through which He can suffer and work except the hearts and bodies of those who are His dwelling place. Through them He does His intercessory work on earth, and they become intercessors by reason of the Intercessor within them. It is real life to which He calls them, the very same kind of life in lesser measure, which the Savior Himself lived on earth.

"But before He can lead a chosen vessel into such a life of intercession, He first has to deal to the bottom with all that is natural. Love of money, personal ambition, natural affection for parents and loved ones, the appetites of the body, the love of life itself, all that makes even a converted man live unto himself, for his own comfort or advantage, for his own advancement, even for his own circle of friends, has to go to the cross. It is no theoretical death, but a real crucifixion with Christ, such as only the Holy Ghost Himself can make actual in the experience of His servant. Both as a crisis and process, Paul's testimony must be made ours: 'I have been and still am crucified with Christ.' The self must be released from itself to become the agent of the Holy Ghost.

"As crucifixion proceeds, intercession begins. By inner burdens, by calls to outward obediences, the Spirit begins to live His own life of love and sacrifice for a lost world through His cleansed channel. We see it in Rees Howell's life. We see it at its greatest height in the Scriptures. . . .

"But intercession is more than the Spirit sharing His groaning with us, and living His life of sacrifice for the world through us. It is the Spirit gaining His ends of abundant grace. If the intercessor knows identification and agony, he also knows authority. It is the law of the corn of wheat and the harvest: 'if it die, it bringeth forth much fruit.'"

The biography cites many graphic stories wherein the intercessor shares with the reader his experiences and growth in this wonderful ministry. Our space is limited, but anyone may find great enlargement of soul through reading the personal life story of Rees Howells. In a very abbreviated sketch in *They Knew Their God,* Vol. 3, we have taken up, in greater detail, this man's journey with God on the pathway of intercession.

Other Welsh Preachers

Some many years ago now an account was sent to a monthly magazine, *Y Drysorfa,* telling of other Welsh preachers who knew the pathway to the secret place of the Most High. We quote:

"Look at the seraphic Robert Roberts, Clynnog, rolling on the floor of the hay-loft, weeping and praying. Why is the poor man in such agony? He is starting on one of his preaching journeys, and is anxious lest the Spirit of God be not with him to convert the world and edify the saints. His study is not a poor one, when we remember the times; but the Bible expositions and books are not sufficient, in his estimation, without the Spirit of God.

"Go to the Association at Llanerch-y-medd, and see the effect of this agonizing in the hay-loft. The hunchback stands on the pavement in front of the Bull Inn, like the angel of God, and in the flood of Divine influences, he lifts up his eyes and hands to Heaven, saying 'Enough, Lord; withhold Thine hand; I can stand no more!'

"Observe Mr. Williams, Lledrod, a scholar and good linguist, and see him on his knees beside the black hedges. It is there he finds the materials of his sermons. Morgan Howells disappears from his family on Saturday night. On Sunday morning he wakes them up early, and calls for his horse. He is ready to go and preach His Master, for he believes that He will go with him.

"The great William Roberts, of Amlwch, would be in a cloud of gloom and depression, struggling with God, before delivering those sermons that swept over the devil's forces like a mighty overwhelming wind. And Mr. Rees, who will ever be remembered with endearment and reverence, whose ministry opened and searched the recesses of my heart many a time—what is he about, and bending on his knees again! He has received a message from God to sinners, and he prays that he may be in the hands of God to deliver it effectively."

AMERICAN PREACHERS
Jonathan Edwards

In the early days of America's history, there were a number of outstanding men of prayer. Jonathan Edwards, through his writings and revival experiences, has become one of the better known among these ministers. The secret of his great usefulness may be found in the way in which he spent time with God until he knew Him as an intimate. Edwards' wife, after some twenty years or more, came into a deep and rich experience with God which delivered her from legality, and changed the flow of grace into her soul from intermittent to constant. She, too, now became an habitual learner at the feet of Christ, and the fields surrounding their home witnessed her profound communion with her Savior.

Jonathan Edwards, at the beginning of his Christian life, adopted this resolution: "Resolved very much to exercise myself in this all my life long; namely, with the greatest openness of which I am capable to declare my ways to God and lay open my soul to Him. . . temptations, difficulties, sorrows, fears, hopes, desires, and everything and every circumstance."

"He made a secret of his private devotions," observed Dr. Hopkins, one of his biographers, "and therefore they cannot be particularly known; though there is much evidence that he was punctual, constant, and frequent in secret prayer and set apart times for serious, devout meditations on spiritual and eternal things as part of his religious exercises.

"It appears from his diary that his stated seasons of private prayer were, from his youth, three times a day, in his journeys as well as at home. He was, as far as can be known, much on his knees alone, and in devout reading of God's Word and meditation upon it. And his constant, solemn converse with God in these exercises of secret religion made his face to shine, as it were, before others."

For three days before he delivered his famous sermon, "Sinners in the Hands of an Angry God," Jonathan Edwards had not closed his eyes in sleep, praying over and over again, "God give me New England."

70

Jonathan Edwards gives us, out of his own experience, a correct picture of walking with God. He says:

"I had vehement longings of soul after God and Christ, and after more holiness, wherewith my heart seemed to be full and ready to break, which often brought to my mind the words of the Psalmist, 'My soul breaketh for the longing . . . it hath.' I often felt a longing and lamenting in my heart that I had not turned to God sooner, that I might have had more time to grow in grace.

"My mind was greatly fixed in divine things, year after year, often walking alone in the woods and in solitary places for meditation, soliloquy, and prayer and converse with God; and it was always my manner at such times to sing forth my contemplation. I was almost constantly in ejaculatory prayer, wherever I was. Prayer seemed to be natural to me, as the breath by which the inward burning of my heart had vent.

"The delights which I now felt in the things of religion were of an exceedingly different kind from what I ever enjoyed before, and what I had no more notion of when a boy than one born blind has of pleasant and beautiful colors. They were of a more inward, pure, soul-animating and refreshing nature. Those former delights never reached the heart and did not arise from sight of the divine excellency of the things of God, or any taste of soul-satisfying and life-giving good there is in them."

O God, Thou art far other than men have dreamed and taught,
Unspoken in all language, unpictured in all thought.
Thou God art God—he only knows what that great Name must be
Whose raptured heart within him burns, because he walks with Thee.
—G. Tersteegen.

The Tennents

Jonathan Edwards was a close friend of the Tennents, another very godly family of ministers who influenced the life of early America in a surprising manner. Arthur Belden, biographer of George Whitefield, says of the Tennents: "The elder Tennent had founded a school at Neshaminy, not far from the city, for ministerial students. This 'Log College,' as it was called, is now Princeton University, and 'became the parent of every Presbyterian College and theological seminary in America.' Tennent's son, Gilbert, minister at Brunswick, a man of terrific though somber oratory, who imitated the scanty, rough dress of a John the Baptist, was also an apostle of the new faith. He threw in his lot enthusiastically with the movement which Whitefield's preaching had launched, and accompanied the latter on his visit from Philadelphia to New York."

The relationship between Whitefield and Gilbert Tennent was similar to that of David and Jonathan. But when it came to preaching with unction and earnestness, Whitefield felt like a babe in Christ in comparison to Tennent, who had a real depth of understanding of the breadth of redemption in its ability to save sinful men and women. Listening to one of Tennent's sermons, Whitefield, himself a mighty orator, said that he was "a son of thunder who must either convert or enrage hypocrites. Never before heard I such a searching sermon. He went to the bottom indeed, and did not daub with untempered mortar. He convinced me more and more that we can preach the Gospel of Christ no further than we have experienced the power of it in our own hearts. I found what a *babe* and *novice* I was in the things of God."

We read of one of the Tennents that on one occasion, when he was engaged in secret devotion, so overpowering was the revelation of God which opened upon his soul, and with augmenting intensity of effulgence as he prayed, that at length he recoiled from the intolerable joy as from a pain, and besought God to withhold from him further manifestations of His glory. He said, "Shall Thy servant see Thee and live?"

A. B. Earle

The Baptist evangelist, A. B. Earle, relates how a night of prayer revolutionized his spiritual life and ministry: "I went home and shut myself in my room, resolved to spend the night in prayer if necessary. O, the struggle of that night! Hour after hour I wrestled alone with God. My heart had been full of coldness, and I not aware of it.

"No wonder the churches had not come up to the work! I renewedly and repeatedly gave myself to the Savior, determined not to let the angel depart until my heart was filled and melted with the love of Jesus. (Gen. 32:1-28).

"Towards morning the victory came! The ice was all broken, melted, and carried away; the warmth and glow of my 'first love' filled my heart; the current of feeling was changed and deepened; the joy of salvation was restored.

"In the morning I went out, took the unconverted by the hand, and said the same things as in days previous; but now they were melted to tears over their sin and danger."

He later tells how a time of united prayer brought in the Kingdom:

"An evangelist had just closed a four weeks' meeting, and said, 'The revival is at an end; we can go no further.' I stopped in town to rest a day or two on the way to a meeting, and was asked to preach. The minute I got in I could see that the net was full of fish, but there was not power enough to pull it to shore. And I said: 'Now, there is that double parlor, and we are going in there to spend the whole of this night in prayer, if Jesus does not answer sooner. You may rely on it, He will answer when He has got something He can use.' One after another we poured out our souls until half-past two in the morning, when Christ seemed to walk in among us, saying: 'My children, I have got prayer that I can use, and you can put your heads on your pillow and go to sleep.' I went home and slept soundly.

"That night God sent conviction like a chain-shot of lightning to the heart of Judge ____. He was a bold sinner—the leaning-post of all the sinners in the town—and he was converted. There was another prominent man in the place, and as soon as he heard the judge was converted, he came and cursed us all, and said: 'Judge ____ has made a fool of himself.' I said: 'Let the man curse; he will pray pretty soon.' The Spirit took away the leaning-post, and swept like a tornado.

"In three or four days all the prayers that were in the golden vials were used up. Fifty of us went to the vestry and prayed till past midnight, till Christ came and told us to go to rest. A third night two hundred of us prayed again to fill the golden vials, and the revival swept like a tornado, and one hundred and fifty men—hard solid men—in that town were converted."

J. A. Bryan of Birmingham

The following is a brief sketch of a Presbyterian preacher whose prayerful life wielded a powerful influence in a large, American city. It is written by Harry Denham, Secretary of Evangelism for the Methodist Church, who was personally acquainted with this unusual man:

"In Birmingham, Alabama, where I was born and lived for forty-five years, the best-known man was not the mayor of the city; nor the editor of the great daily newspaper; nor the president of the Tennessee Coal, Iron, and Railroad Company, which employed 30,000 persons;

73

nor the president of the great bank. The best-known man was a humble Presbyterian preacher, J. A. Bryan by name but whom everyone called Brother Bryan.

"He came to Birmingham as a young man to a young city. He did not come to mine our coal or dig our ore, or to manufacture our steel, or to build sky-scrapers, but, as William L. Stidger of Boston University School of Theology, said, 'He came to be a fool for Christ.' This is the best way to describe him. Others were fools for gold, for pleasure, for social standing, for education, and political achievements; but Brother Bryan was a fool for Christ.

"He was known as a man of prayer. When his tired body died, the citizens of Birmingham erected a monument to his memory. It was a stone carving of Brother Bryan on his knees, praying. That is how the people of the great industrial city desired to remember him.

"He prayed with my mother and father before I was born. At midnight at the streetcar barn one could find Brother Bryan praying with the motor-men and conductors as they came to the barn on their last run. He prayed with the men in the railroad shops and other places early in the morning before they started the day's work.

"He ministered to more people in our city in their sorrows than any other minister. He was known to all persons, regardless of their class, creed, color, or financial standing.

"One day he and I stood on Second Avenue and Twentieth Street, the busiest corner of the city. There he prayed for men and women who were in trouble and need. Another day I saw him take off his old black hat and flag a limousine approaching him. The beautiful car stopped, as all cars did for Brother Bryan. Some charming ladies were seated in the back seat. Brother Bryan said to them, 'May I pray with you?' They consented, as all persons did at his request. He prayed a short prayer, told the ladies goodbye, and waved the chauffeur on his way.

"He conducted many services for those whose bodies were dead. Sometimes he would be the only person at the service and would ride in the hearse with the funeral director. Many times there were young preachers to help him with the service.

"Brother Bryan always proclaimed the Gospel at a funeral service. He said that was the only time some persons had the opportunity to hear a sermon. He always asked the assisting minister to pray. One time he called on a young man to pray. The young man prayed and prayed and prayed. He kept on praying. Finally he said 'Amen.' Brother

Bryan turned to him and said, 'Son, if you would pray more often, you would not be so far behind in your praying.'

"Brother Bryan would telephone persons and ask if he could pray with them over the telephone. They were happy to say yes. He would pray a short prayer, say amen and goodbye, and call another person.

"I could tell you many stories about Brother Bryan.

"One day his tired heart stopped. His body was taken to the cemetery, not in a hearse, but on a city fire-truck because he was the chaplain for the city. Along the three miles from his church to the cemetery, thousands of persons lined both sides of the streets and wept unashamedly as Birmingham's Man of Prayer was laid to rest in beautiful Elmwood Park. He prayed when he lived in the days of his flesh. I am sure he is praying as he lives in the spirit."

—(Used by permission as published in the *Wesleyan Methodist.*)

Asa Mahan

Asa Mahan, president of Oberlin University for fifteen years, experienced a striking display of God's power in answer to a Spirit-inspired prayer. "I had an appointment," he said, "during the season of afflictive drought, to preach in one of the churches of the city where I lived one Sabbath morning. As we came to our carriage, I said to my wife, 'There is not the remotest probability that it will rain today. I will, therefore, carry in the robe which we usually take with us,' and did so.

"When I kneeled to pray before that congregation, I had no more expectation that it would rain that day outside than inside the house of God. When I began to pray about the drought, however, a power came upon me which rendered that prayer a wonder to myself and the congregation. The Monday's issue of our daily paper contained this statement: 'The preacher in one of our churches prayed very fervently yesterday morning that it might rain, and his congregation were drenched with rain on going home at the close of that service.'

"I can never tell when 'the spirit of grace and of supplication,' in that form, shall be poured upon me. Nor do I feel under obligation to have such experience whenever I pray. All that I can do, or feel bound to do, is to leave my heart open, and let the Spirit intercede in it as and when He chooses. This I do say, however, that when the Spirit does thus intercede, I always obtain the specific object for which I pray. Nor can anyone pray under the intercessory power of the Spirit without the hearer, as well as himself, marking the peculiarity of prayer.

"Hence it is that, for many years past, my students, in times of drought, for example, have been accustomed to say, 'We shall have rain now. Did you mark our President's prayer?' Nor were they ever disappointed."

A. B. Simpson

A.B. Simpson was the founder of the Christian Missionary Alliance Church and literally prayed hundreds of missionaries into the spiritually barren wastes of the earth to sow and reap for the Lord of the harvest.

"A guest in the home of A. B. Simpson rose early one morning to take a walk. As he passed the open door of his host's study he saw him seated at his desk. He noticed Dr. Simpson had finished reading his Bible and had begun to pray. However, he did not drop to his knees beside the desk, nor did he bow his head and close his eyes. Instead, he reached out and pulled toward him a small globe. Turning it slowly, he prayed aloud for all the lost multitudes as the various countries passed beneath his fingers.

"Suddenly, unmindful of the guest who was watching, Dr. Simpson put his arms around the globe and hugged it to him. He bent over the globe, and wept so that his tears struck the top of the globe, divided, and ran down over each side—until the whole world was wet with his tears of compassion!

"Missionaries whom he had trained and sent forth had planted the seed of the Word of God in hearts around the globe—now the elderly mission leader sought to 'water' that seed with tears of compassion. God still seeks intercessors who will pray with that kind of spirit."—Unknown.

"Our greatest work is prayer," said Dr. Simpson. "Real prayer in the Holy Ghost is as rare as it is mighty. It means great sufferings and brings us into fellowship with the Lord in all the burdens which He is ever bearing for His people before the throne. Such prayer is an actual force. Oh, for the golden pipes to carry the oil from the living trees to the lamps of God! Oh, for the incense bearers to ever present to Heaven the golden vials which are the prayers of the saints and bring the great consummation! In these solemn times we expect God to lay upon us unusual burdens of intercession. Let Him find us responsible and understanding what the will of the Lord is."

"Intercession" we are told, "was the secret of his successful public ministry. No one knew this so well as he, for in *The King's Business* he says: 'I have noticed that those who claim and expect souls for God have them given to them; and, for myself, I never dare to preach to the unsaved without first claiming alone with God the real birth of souls, and receiving the assurance of His quickening and new-creating life distinctly for this end. If I fail to do this, I am usually disappointed in the results of the meeting.'"

A Tennessee Preacher

"We had a great preacher in Tennessee once, who lived only three years after he commenced to preach. He was, perhaps, the greatest man for his day that was ever produced in the West. Hundreds and thousands were converted under his ministry.

"One day his brother said to him, 'Sterling, how is it that you are so much more successful in preaching the Gospel than others? We preach the same doctrines. We understand them as well as you. We are in earnest. How is it that you succeed, and I do not?'

"He modestly, and with hesitancy, said, 'Brother, the secret all lies here: Before I go to the pulpit I go to God in prayer, and if I can feel an assurance there that God will help me, I always succeed. But if I fail to have that assurance, I am just like the rest of you.'

"I tell you, brother preachers, if we had more prayer in the closet, preparatory to preaching, more souls would be converted under our ministry."—Rev. John B. M'Ferrin.

Peter Jackson

"A survey of the great revivals of the past shows that in their beginnings it was prayer and work and obedience that was written on their price tags.

"Peter Jackson of over a century and a half ago was a preacher who built himself a little hut in the Pennsylvania woods near his home. His practice was to slip away to this hut to pray when he found a few moments to spare. More and more he prayed for revival in his community until he was called 'the praying elder.'

"Some nights he would stay on his knees all night long, praying for revival at any cost. This prayer vigil he kept before the throne of God for months. Then revival came. It swept his own church, his city, and his state. Indeed, it is known in some church records as the revival of eighteen hundred. One man's prayer started it. He paid the price."

—Fletcher Clark Spruce.

G. D. Watson

We, the authors of this book, owe very much to the writings of George Watson. We had both, while quite young, received a vital infilling of the Holy Spirit, and our instruction as to how to receive Him was very detailed. But we had never had any instruction on how to retain Him, nor what to expect in the way of trials and testings. Hence, we were deeply distressed at times to know just what was the meaning of those strange crosses which we were encountering in our Christian pathway. Someone introduced us to the writings of G. D. Watson, and oh, what light he threw upon many of the interior crucifixions which one inevitably meets with in their onward course in knowing God! He writes for the sanctified, and understands the peculiar tests which they must pass through in order to become conformed to the image of Christ.

We pass on several experiences of G. D. Watson in order that you might realize how prayer in the Spirit differs so from perfunctory prayer which can often-times make us self-righteous and Pharisaical. The Spirit was given to help our infirmities for none of us know how to pray as we should but He stands by to initiate a burden, and then sustain us as we carry that prayer burden through to fruition. We share several of Mr. Watson's experiences with you that you might have great expectations from God in praying in the Holy Ghost.

The Divine Pull

"Oftentimes, when I have been traveling on the cars, going at the rate of thirty or forty miles per hour, I have felt the train give a sudden pull, because the engineer had turned on more steam to increase the speed to fifty miles per hour. To one who travels a good deal, and has a keen sense of motion, every movement of the train can be readily detected. I can detect when the train turns in the least to the right or left, or the slightest pressure of the air-brake on the wheels, or the least increase of speed.

"This sensitiveness to the motion of a train should be realized in the spiritual life. If we keep in a very humble and crucified state of mind, and in unbroken fellowship with the Holy Spirit, the interior sensibilities of the soul will be just as keen as those of the body. We can detect the least slackening of speed, or the least veering to the right or left. Blessed be God, we can be conscious when the heavenly Engineer turns on more spiritual pressure.

"It will often happen in secret prayer, when all the faculties of the soul are open to the sway of the Spirit, that we can feel a Divine pull upon our hearts, a sudden yearning of the soul after God stronger than hitherto; a deep, sweet passion for Christ takes hold upon the fountains of desire; a longing, an intense craving to be just like Jesus pervades the whole mind. At such moments we feel magnetized. We are conscious that an infinite lodestone is drawing our desires, affections, choices, and imaginations up into the brightness and sweetness of God.

"Such moments are worth more than we can conjecture. We should make everything of them. When the Spirit gives us such gentle pulls to Himself, we should open the throttle-valve of the heart to its uttermost. Let the tears flow. Let hours, if need be, glide away unheeded, even if it is midnight. Let the Divine nature open its great, sweet splendors to our mind. Let us push our way at such times into the very bosom of Jesus. Let us take the hint of His drawing, and make deep and passionate love with Him. At such times let us spread before Him all our unselfish longings for the salvation of souls, special petitions for relatives and friends and foes, for great Revivals, for mission-fields. While these sweet seraphic winds blow down upon us, let us stretch every sail, and oil the bottom of our ships and make all the speed possible. Many a season of prayer is without fruit because the 'Amen' is said just about the time the blessed Spirit is getting His fingers on the heart-strings for a heavenly pull.

"In the past few months, more than ever in my past life, I am learning to detect the gentle movements of the Holy Spirit in my soul in prayer. Sometimes I begin praying with a weary, dull feeling. My thoughts seem dry, my affections seem becalmed, and this dryness lingers for ten or twenty minutes, but by fixing my thoughts on God and asking Him to breathe in me the very prayer which will most please the Father, and then by patiently waiting and pleading the infinite merit of my elder Brother, by and by the brightness begins to come. The heart is melted. Tears of love and thanksgiving flow. An inexpressible sweetness settles into all my being. Then all difficulties, all sorrows, all hardships, all burdens, all loneliness, all anxiety of every sort and degree, sink away below the horizon.

"I feel it pays immensely to watch the movements of the Spirit. . . .Oh, that we may get so intimate with the Holy Spirit as to take His slightest hint, and feel His gentlest pull, and always yield a loving response to His wishes! What an infinite compliment that our heavenly Father should be willing to indicate His thoughts and His desires toward us through the emotions of His Spirit! If we respond to His gentle pulls in prayer, it will enable us to more readily detect any warning or premonition which He may give us of approaching danger or of the blessedness of some golden opportunity."—*Soul Food.*

Praying For An Enemy

"I am convinced we have far too shallow views of that command to pray for our enemies. It means vastly more than to say, 'God bless our foes.' It means that we are to take them on our heart in good earnest, and intercede for them, particularly, lovingly, perseveringly—pray for them till out of a loving heart we can unite their highest welfare with our own.

"I have been blessed all my life with a few enemies; at a few periods in my life with a great many, and sometimes they have been exceedingly bitter. But in reviewing the past, I notice that I have had the fewest enemies and the most popularity when I was the least spiritual and the farthest away from God. When I have had deepest fellowship with Christ, I have been the most misunderstood by religious people and the most intensely hated by bad people. I can recall many seasons when I felt it a necessity to pray especially both for positive enemies and for Christian people, who had greatly injured me, while they did not intend to be my foes.

"One such circumstance occurred in the early summer of 1895. A certain very bitter enemy had done many things to greatly damage both me and my family. I had often prayed for him in my secret devotions, but one day I felt drawn to go off alone into a forest and spend some hours in pleading to God for him and his family. At the beginning of my prayer, I tried to exercise great charity for the man by putting myself in his place, and looking at my own miserable self from his standpoint. But the Spirit soon showed me that was the human way, and not the Divine. It came to me that what I needed was to love that man with the identical love that Jesus had for him; to pity, sympathize with, and feel toward him exactly as God felt, up to my capacity. I was to be a living vessel in such union with the Holy Spirit that Jesus could love him through me, and pour His Divine love through my affections.

"It was revealed to me that in order to love him as Christ loved, I must utterly abandon my being to the Holy Spirit, for the purpose of becoming a channel of the perfectly unselfish, impartial, disinterested, tender, and boundless compassion of God. I complied with the suggestion of the Spirit, and before I had prayed an hour the fountains of my soul were broken up; my tears flowed like rain. I felt a warm, soft love for him. All his welfare of body and soul, all his family, all his temporal and eternal interests, became very precious in my sight.

"As I continued to plead with God for his soul's salvation, and for all his welfare in detail, suddenly the Spirit opened to my mind what a lovely Christian that man would make if he was thoroughly washed in Jesus' blood and filled with the Holy Spirit. I seemed to see his soul and all his gifts and powers, now so perverted by sin—how lovely they would be if transformed by Divine grace! As I viewed him under the possibilities of saving grace, he seemed transfigured in my vision. I then prayed that I might feel a Christ-like grief for any trouble that might befall him. From that moment it has been easy and sweet to pray for him, and I never think of him except with a peculiarly tender love.

"A few months after, that man had a great calamity which brought pain and sadness to my heart; yet I was accused of praying the misfortune upon him. Our neighbors and acquaintances can never really know what is in our hearts till that Great Day. It is infinitely more essential that we actually love our fellows than that we convince them of our love. If Jesus was unable to convince men of His love to them, are we greater than He? It is the deep reality of having the Christ-love flow through us to everybody that we need, far more than the success of showing it to people. I find the more I pray for anyone, the easier it is for me to think well of him, and to look at his conduct in the most favorable light.

"Not only must we pray long and fervently for our positive foes, but pray much for religious people who are cold and severe to us; for if we do not keep our hearts warm and pure, and very tender to everybody on earth, we lose that sweet sense of oneness with Jesus which is worth more than all the friendships of creatures. It is not my calling to make people love me; it is my great business to have perfect union with the Holy Spirit, and to love all with God's love, whether they love or have confidence in me or not."—*Soul Food*.

Marvelous Answer to Prayer

"During the year 1895, the Lord permitted me to have in my life and experience many very wonderful answers to prayer. I wish now to give an account of only one among a great number:

"It is well known that the orange groves in Florida were nearly all killed in January, 1895, so that my property, from which I expected a support, was all ruined. I was divinely kept from even a thought of a murmur. I fasted and prayed many days, and made a solemn covenant with God. First I would ask help of no one except the Lord. Second, that I would not go any deeper in debt. Third, that I would very rigidly give God one-tenth of all He gave to me. My faith had a few testing seasons, but I never lacked, and I was never out of cash money. The infinitely tender dealings of God for the year, in spiritual and physical matters, would fill a book. Here is only one.

"I had more urgent need for money coming due in November. I knew I had no way to get the money but by prayer, so all through September and October I prayed much for the funds, and I observed several days of fasting. I was kept in perfect peace, yet intense looking to God. During the last week in October, a poor, sanctified widow fifteen hundred miles from me, and who had never seen me, wrote to me that she was very powerfully impressed of the Spirit, to spend a whole day in prayer for my temporal supplies, and that God spoke into her heart that He would supply my needs. I needed one hundred dollars by November 10th, and another hundred in December, but my little prayer only took in the first hundred.

"On the 6th of November, after supper, just before beginning the weekly holiness meeting in my house, I was walking in the library, talking with the Lord of my deep need. Suddenly the Holy Ghost opened up to my mind a fresh and strong view of the Fatherly provision of God for me. My whole soul was melted into love and peace. Tears of joy flowed down my face. There was something like a voice talking in my heart, which said, 'Money is nothing to Me. It is only My wrapping-paper, and is inexhaustible. Just give Me continually your warmest love and perfect obedience, and I will attend to your finances.'

"With these words in my mind, I felt that my prayer was answered. In four more days the money would be needed, and I did not have my mind on anybody on earth to supply it. On the 9th I received a letter from a sanctified business man, several thousand miles away, saying that he 'felt a strong impulse to send me a check for over two hundred dollars.' The receipt of the check did not surprise me at all, for my faith was expecting God to do something. I walked into the forest and sat down on a log, and just gazed for an hour at the great and loving God, and adored His matchless love and the reality of His personal presence. I did not know which to admire most, the movement of the Holy Ghost on the widow to pray, or on the dear brother to send the money. And then to see the accuracy of the Lord's time-table, that the supply should reach me just on time to a day. I at once took out one-tenth for the Lord."—*Soul Food.*

"Every man's character depends on his prayers. It will be seen, at the final judgment, that all holy character will be in exact conformity to what has been the prayer-life of the individual. There is a history to prayer which is so interior and spiritual that we ourselves are not able to analyze it, or to mark its various degrees, and it would take the intelligence of an angel to write out the history of the prayers of God's people. Doubtless, it is this that will be manifested at the time that the prayers of all saints are brought to their culmination and completion."
—*God's Eagles.*

We conclude this chapter with an exhortation from Philip Brooks: "O my dear friends, there is not one of us that can live without praying. We all know that. But praying is not 'saying our prayers,' not shuffling through a few petitions morning and evening, nor clamoring with imperious voices before God's presence, setting up our own will, however earnestly and vehemently, against His. 'Lord, teach us to pray,' we ask: and the first answer is, 'If ye abide in me and my words abide in you,' then ye shall pray successfully. We must be Christians first. We must enter into the new life, and, once there, prayer will grow wonderfully easy; as easy to pray on earth, 'Lord Jesus, have mercy upon me,' as it will be to praise in Heaven, 'Thou art worthy, O Lord, for thou hast redeemed us.'"

MORE AMERICAN PREACHERS

Edward Payson

The wonder of the next world will be to trace the far-reaching influences of men and women of prayer who thought it no waste of time to spend hours and even days in the study of the Word of God and in communion with Father, Son, and Holy Ghost. The New England preacher, Edward Payson, Congregational in denomination, was certainly one who evidenced such a lack of confidence in the flesh that he insisted upon staying in the Divine Presence until infused with exalted views of God's holiness and majesty. He could then minister to others not in words of man's wisdom but in demonstration of the Spirit and of power.

One day, his four or five year-old daughter, Elizabeth, rushed unexpectedly into her father's room and found him prostrate upon his face in audience with God. He was so lost in his devotions that he did not know of her entrance. She was nine years of age when her father died, but "his influence had penetrated to her inmost being. Speaking of this scene a short time before her death, she remarked that it had influenced her ever since." As an authoress, Elizabeth Prentiss gave to the public her book, *Stepping Heavenward,* and as a godly minister's wife, continued the prayer pattern engraved upon her childhood memory.

Let our own lives of prayer be improved as we meditate on the private prayer life of the Rev. Payson as depicted in *Lectures on Revivals* by E. N. Kirk: "His view of prayer was that, for himself, he could not live safely without incessant prayer; not always on his knees, but always staying very near the mercy-seat, and visiting it very frequently. Such was his estimate of the prayers of believers, that he aimed to form little groups of four or six persons, who should meet before service on Sunday morning, to pray for a blessing on the minister and his labors that day.

"Thus his diary describes his own praying: 'Was enabled to agonize in prayer for myself and people, and to make intercession with

unutterable groaning. My heart and flesh cried out for the living God.'
He believed that nothing brought more glory to God than social prayer.

"And probably the indirect influence of his public prayers was even greater than that of his preaching. They doubtless prevailed with God, and they certainly affected men very profoundly.

"To this subject the attention of theological students must yet be turned, as it probably has not yet been. It is not liturgies we need, but the spirit of prayer, obtained, as Payson obtained it, by close communion with God."

E. M. Bounds, that great prophet of prayer, said that "Payson wore the hard-wood boards into grooves where his knees pressed so often and so long."

One of Payson's biographers wrote: "His continuing instant in prayer, be his circumstances what they might, is the most noticeable fact in his history, and points out the duty of all who would rival his eminency. To his ardent and persevering prayers must no doubt be ascribed in a great measure his distinguished and almost uninterrupted success."

In *The Hidden Life of Prayer* D. M. M'Intyre says: "The biographer of Payson observes that 'prayer was preeminently the business of his life,' and he himself used to aver that he pitied that Christian who could not enter into the meaning of the words, 'groanings which cannot be uttered.' It was recorded of him that 'he studied theology on his knees.' Is it any wonder that he was permitted to point a great multitude of men to Christ?"

Mr. Payson warns his readers about the opposition from Satan that one must expect if he would persevere in this art of prayer.

"On maintaining the daily performance of closet duties the fate of the whole battle will turn. This your great adversary well knows. He knows that if he can beat you out of the closet, he will have you in his own power. You will be in the situation of an army cut off from supplies and reinforcements and will be obliged either to capitulate or to surrender at discretion.

"He will, therefore, leave no means untried to drive or draw you from the closet. And it will be hard work to maintain that post against him and your own heart. On some occasions he will probably assail you with more violence when you attempt to read or pray than at any other time, and thus try to persuade you that prayer is rather injurious than beneficial. Again, he will withdraw and be quiet lest, if he should distress you with his temptations, you might be driven to the Throne of Grace for help. If he can prevail upon us to be careless and stupid, he rarely will distress us. He will not disturb a false peace because it is a peace of which he is the author. But if he cannot succeed in lulling us to sleep, he will do all in his power to distress us.

"And when he is permitted to do this, and the Holy Spirit withdraws His sensible aid and consolations; when, though we cry and shout, God seems to shut out our prayers, it is by no means easy to be constant in secret duties. Indeed, it is always most difficult to attend to them when they are most necessary."

Quite striking is his description of the man who neglects prayer: "The man who refuses or neglects to pray, who regards prayer not as a privilege but as a wearisome and needless task, practically says, in the most unequivocal manner: 'I am not dependent upon God. I want nothing that He can give; and therefore I will not come to Him or ask any favor at His hands. I will not ask Him to crown my exertions with success, for I am able and determined to be architect of my own fortune.

"'I will not ask His presence and aid in the hour of death, for I can meet and grapple, unsupported, with the king of terrors and enter, undaunted and alone, any unknown world into which He may usher me.' Such is the language of all who neglect prayer."

His advice to a fellow-minister was: "My dear brother, I cannot insist on this too much. Prayer is the first thing, the second thing, and the third thing necessary for a minister, especially in scenes of revival. The longer you live in the ministry, the more deeply, I am persuaded, you will be convinced of this."

E. M. Bounds

Edward McKendrie Bounds served several churches of importance in St. Louis and other places in the South. For eight years he was editor of the *St. Louis Christian Advocate* and for four years was associate editor of the *Nashville Christian Advocate*. Later he largely gave up his ministry in the pulpit in order to encourage the ministry to prayer, especially early morning prayer. His life was a benediction to all, and his books on prayer are still selling. The following extracts are taken from his book, *Power Through Prayer*:

"It may be put down as a spiritual axiom that in every truly successful ministry prayer is an evident and controlling force—evident and controlling in the life of the preacher, evident and controlling in the deep spirituality of his work. A ministry may be a very thoughtful ministry without prayer; the preacher may secure fame and popularity without prayer; the whole machinery of the preacher's life and work may run without the oil of prayer or with scarcely enough to grease one cog; but no ministry can be a spiritual one securing holiness in the preacher and in his people, without prayer being made an evident and controlling force.

"The preacher that prays indeed puts God into the work. God does not come into the preacher's work as a matter of course or on general principles. But He comes by prayer and special urgency. A prayerful ministry is the only ministry that brings the preacher into sympathy with the people. . . . A prayerful ministry is the only ministry qualified for the high offices and responsibilities of the preacher. Colleges, learning, books, theology, preaching cannot make a preacher, but praying does. The apostles' commission to preach was a blank till filled up by the Pentecost which praying brought.

"A prayerful minister has passed beyond the man of mere affairs, of secularities, of pulpit attractiveness; passed beyond the ecclesiastical organizer or general into a sublime and mightier region, the region of the spiritual. . . . God is with him. His ministry is not projected on worldly or surface principles. He is deeply stored with and deeply schooled in the things of God. His long, deep communing with God about his people and the agony of his wrestling spirit have crowned him as a prince in the things of God. The iciness of the mere professional has long since melted under the intensity of his praying.

"The superficial results of many a ministry, the deadness of others, are to be found in the lack of praying. No ministry can succeed without much praying, and this praying must be fundamental, ever abiding, ever increasing. The text, the sermon, should be the result of prayer. The study should be bathed in prayer, all its duties impregnated with prayer, its whole spirit the spirit of prayer. 'I am sorry that I have prayed so little,' was the deathbed regret of one of God's chosen ones, a sad and remorseful regret for a preacher. 'I want a life of greater, deeper, truer prayer,' said the late Archbishop Tait. So may we all say, and this may we all secure.

"God's true preachers have been distinguished by one great feature: they were men of prayer. Differing often in many things, they have always had a common center. . . . These men prayed not occasionally, not a little at regular or at odd times; but they so prayed that their prayers entered into and shaped their characters. They so prayed as to affect their own lives and the lives of others. They so prayed as to make the history of the Church and influence the current of the times. They spent much time in prayer, not because they marked the shadow on the dial or the hands on the clock, but because it was to them so momentous and engaging a business that they could scarcely give over."

Wilbur Chapman

"If we would do more pleading with God we would not have to do so much pleading with men. It is not great preaching that we need but great praying! It is power, power from on high that we need today. I desire to impress this upon every layman who reads these lines. It is one of Satan's wiles to lead the church to throw all responsibility for the possession of this spiritual dynamite and success in spiritual work upon the minister, the membership indulging themselves in worldliness and unspirituality. At Pentecost, it was Peter and the whole church filled with the Holy Ghost that harvested the three thousand souls, and not Peter, alone, facing the mob with a breaking heart.

"Wilbur Chapman once said that, when he went to Philadelphia to be pastor of Wanamaker's church, after his first sermon an old man met him in front of the pulpit, and said, 'You are pretty young to be pastor of this great church. We have always had older pastors. I am afraid you won't succeed. But you preach the Gospel, and I am going to help you all I can.'

"'I looked at him,' said Dr. Chapman, 'and said to myself, "He is a crank."'

"But the old man continued, 'I am going to pray for you, that you may have the Holy Spirit power upon you, and two others have covenanted to join with me.'

"Said Mr. Chapman, 'I did not feel so bad when I learned that he was going to pray for me. The three became ten, the ten became twenty, and the twenty became fifty, and the fifty became two hundred, who met before every service to pray that the Holy Spirit might come upon me. In another room the eighteen elders knelt so close around me to pray for me that I could put my hands and touch them on all sides.

"'I always went into my pulpit feeling that I would have the anointing in answer to the prayers of the two hundred and eighteen men. I do not see how the average pastor, under average circumstances, preaches at all.'

"O disciples of Christ, remember you have something else to do besides going to church as curious, idle spectators, to be amused and entertained or even instructed. It is your business to pray mightily that the Holy Ghost will clothe your minister with power, and make his words like dynamite to the flinty hearts of sinners.

"If we would obtain this power we must feel deep down in our hearts that nothing can supply its place. Here lies the difficulty of the church in multitudes of instances. She leans upon other things to do the very work which the Holy Spirit was sent into the world to perform. In some cases she will lean upon the minister, his talent, his eloquence, his learning, or his influence. When the church has secured the man of her choice, she sits down to rest. She expects he will build her up. What can a minister do unless he has this power to work with him? If he is as eloquent as Gabriel, not a soul will be saved without this power. The church must feel this and be on her face, and plead with God for the Holy Ghost to work in him.

"It was a church leaning hard on God in prayer for a week, and spending nearly two whole nights in prayer, that brought the Holy Spirit upon their pastor, Livingstone, when he preached the sermon at Shotts that brought five hundred to Jesus. Finney says that it was the praying of 'Father' Nash and Brother Clary and other souls who were walking with God that clothed him with such power from on high that the stoutest sinners were broken down. . . .

"Churches are calling for men of great learning and eloquence instead of men who are deeply baptized with the Holy Ghost. Seminaries of learning are much at fault. They do not stress this enduement as an essential qualification. And so the seminaries of learning and the

89

churches themselves are bringing up a barren ministry to increase the desolation of Zion. O teachers of ministers! O people of God! Lay stress upon the divine anointing!"—A. M. Hills.

J. Wilbur Chapman once came to F. B. Meyer with the question, "What is the matter with me? So many times I seem half empty, and so many times utterly powerless; what is the matter?"

Mr Meyer put his hand on Chapman's shoulder and answered, "Have you ever tried to breathe out three times without breathing in once?"

Thinking it might be some new breathing exercise, Chapman answered, "I do not think I have."

"Well," said Meyer, "try it." So he breathed out once, and then he had to breathe in again.

"Don't you know," said Dr. Meyer, "that you must always breathe in before you breathe out, and that your breathing out is in proportion to your breathing in?"

We must fill the reservoir by prayer and a meditative study of the Word before we can draw out for service.

A. C. Dixon

"One of the most persuasive preachers of some years ago was Dr. A. C. Dixon of U. S. A. To many who sat in darkness his splendid mastery of noble language, his haunting descriptions, his incisive appeals, brought light; yet the early years of his ministry were fraught with disappointment.

"Fresh from his triumphs in the academic circles of his university, he deceived himself into thinking that his learning and eloquence were all that mattered for his success; yet he experienced nothing but failure. To his services came many students bent on mischief, and the preacher's efforts to silence their interruptions were only in vain. All the tricks of oratory, his use of the poets, his reference to science, his application of psychology—all were futile.

"Then came the crisis. Out into the fields alone he went—alone with God. Hours were spent in humiliation, confession, prayer, supplication, intercession; and the power came! That night there were no interruptions. The atmosphere was electric. The power of God was present to heal. A work of grace was begun. The preacher had prevailed through prayer."—Anon.

James Duncan, preaching with great unction and power, was asked what was the secret of such powerful preaching. "The secret," he said, "was thirteen hours of consecutive prayer."

Ezekiel, the prophet, was given a vision regarding the apostasy of Israel and the purging began at the Temple. A man with an inkhorn was told to "go through the midst of the city, through the midst of Jerusalem, and set a mark upon the foreheads of the men that sigh and that cry for all the abominations that be done in the midst thereof." In the vision, God then authorized other men to follow up the work of the man with the inkhorn and not let their eyes spare but to slay those who had not the mark upon their forehead. God commissioned these men to begin at the sanctuary.

We fear that if such a test were to be put today to the priests and ministers of our Western world, that we might well fall upon our face and cry with Ezekiel, "Ah Lord God, wilt thou destroy all the residue of Israel?" Contemporary, popular evangelists and preachers would well come under the wrath of God, because they spend so little time sighing and crying over the materialism and Sodomy of our luxury-minded church members. We have been shocked as we have gone around to discover how little knowledge the average church-going person has of the Bible. They are not even getting the ABC's of the Gospel; the ministers stop with "A" and do not even get to the "B" and "C." We trust that there may be a revival first among those who minister in the pulpits and then among the lay people, that God's judgments will not fall upon our Western nations already taken over by corruption.

The following incident was related in a religious paper some years ago. We fear that if the same canvass were taken in a ministers' gathering today, the response would be even less encouraging.

In a conference of ministers it was once suggested, "Brethren, let us today make confession before God and each other. It will do us good. Will everyone who spends half an hour every day with God in connection with His work, hold up a hand." One hand was held up. "All who spend 15 minutes." Not half of the hands were held up. "All who spend five minutes hold up a hand." All hands were held up. But one man came back afterwards with the confession that he was not quite sure if he spent five minutes in prayer every day. "It is," said he, "a terrible revelation of how little time I spend with God."

Practice the presence of Jesus
    In all that you do and say.
Remember His beautiful promise,
    "I will be with you alway":

In the hush of the early morning,
    Ere the clamoring duties come;
And all through the day with its problems,
    Till the time of the setting sun.

Think of Him always as walking
    Constantly there at your side,
Giving you power and purpose,
    With nothing you'll need to hide.

Then, all through the nights—some sleepless—
    Remember you're not alone.
Practice the presence of Jesus
    Till you reach your heavenly home!
                    —Alice Hansche Mortenson.
                    (Used by permission).

GERMAN PREACHERS

Gerhard Tersteegen

It was in *Mülheim,* Germany, in the beginning of the 1700's, that a twenty-two-year-old business man, Gerhard Tersteegen, vexed with the trivial conversation and pursuits of those around him, left his business in order to retire and be alone with God. He felt unequal to row against the pressures of the world about him and rented a cottage where he could support himself by weaving ribbon silk. Here he was enabled to work in quiet and without molestation with his Bible open before him. He waited upon the Lord, learning deep secrets that are only revealed to such sincere seekers after God.

For five years the youth encountered a period of darkness which surprised and puzzled him, but at twenty-seven he emerged from that gloom into a bright experience after dedicating himself for time and eternity to complete obedience to the Lord Jesus Christ. Like his Master, Whose earthly ministry began when He was thirty years of age, this recluse was forced to leave his solitude. A revival in *Mülheim* called forth all his energies. There were young babes in Christ hungry for the true Bread of Life which they could not get from an unawakened clergy. After wearying efforts feeding souls he would retire for whole days to the neighboring woods where he could regain quietness of soul. Here he wiped away the soil and grime of worldly contact and so could go forth renewed in spirit with bright apprehensions of God.

News travels fast, and there were those who spoke of the help they had received from Tersteegen. Now requests for his services came in from neighboring countries which necessitated much travel. All he had learned in his Arabia was of utmost value.

When he was fifty years of age, a second revival occurred in the nearby district. Another instrument who had been widely used in this ministry was called away and it fell upon this prepared warrior to meet the urgent requirements occasioned by such an awakening. Souls traveled distances to come to hear Tersteegen, the man who had heard from God. Larger premises were secured and even then the crowds could not be contained. They took their seats in open windows and listened from out of doors as they hung upon every word spoken with such unction and power.

In *They Knew Their God*, Vol. 2, we have given a more detailed study of this saintly man, but we add a few extracts from his writings that they might help us to a deeper concept of prayer and that we might come to value very highly time spent alone with God:

"The great importance of perseverance in the exercise of prayer and inward retirement may be sufficiently learnt, next to the experience of it, merely from the tempter's artifices and endeavors to allure us from it, and make us negligent in it. He knows by this delightful exercise alone, his gloomy empire in the soul will necessarily be destroyed, through the imperceptible influx of the light, love, and life of Jesus; and that all the flowers and fruits of the fairest gifts of grace and virtue fade of themselves, if he can only break them off from this their root. Jesus alone is the Mediator and Medium by which divine life and strength can be again imparted to our illegitimate and depraved humanity.

"By the exercise of the prayer of the heart, in which faith, love, hope, etc., concentrate themselves, we are, and continue united to Him, and rooted in Him—the hungering desire and affection, and ardent inclination, being as it were the root, by which we imperceptibly receive from Jesus sap and strength, although we do not always obviously see and feel how it is, and whether it is taking place. O let us pray, and prepare ourselves for retiring within our hearts! The most imperfect prayer is of more advantage than the best diversion from it. The adversary lets us do many things which seem to be good and even incites us to them, only to cause us to neglect prayer.

"My own experience and the experience of others has repeatedly taught me that the tempter especially watches, in the season of abandonment, barrenness, and darkness, to detach the soul from the steadfast exercise of prayer, and to weaken its strength, these being precisely the times when we might be prepared for making the most rapid advancement, and for thoroughly forsaking ourselves, if we only

94

continued firm in enduring the Lord's will, and knew how to submit ourselves entirely to Him."

"God invites us to His lovely fellowship; He purposes preparing our spirits for His habitation and temple, and in this inward sanctuary, we shall behold the beauty of the Lord. O what a mercy! If then the overflowings of the love of God towards our unworthy souls are so exceedingly abundant, we ought also, beloved brother, to be very liberal, and not withhold ourselves, in any respect, from this eternal Good, which seeks to have us solely and wholly for itself."

"God is a placid Being, and dwells in a serene eternity. Therefore thy mind must become like a clear and silent streamlet, in which the glory of God can reflect and portray itself. Hence thou must avoid all disturbance, confusion, and irritation, inwardly and outwardly. There is nothing in the world deserves being troubled about: even thy past faults must only humble, but not disturb thee. 'God is in his holy temple, (Hab. 2:20) let all that is within thee keep silence before him!'"

"He who loves and exercises prayer will, in due time, be gradually translated from self into God—from the impure and imperfect working in his own strength, into a working through God and for God. I only wish that all, from the very commencement of their way, would consider godliness, or the service of God, in a proper light—that is, as happiness and salvation to which we are called, and which God designs to grant unto us; and that the sooner and the more they forsake themselves and the creature by prayer and self-denial, they the sooner approach unto God even though they neither see nor feel it, and consequently become more happy for God Himself is essentially our salvation and our end. The more cordially and completely we live to God, the more happy we become from that moment. O this is so exceedingly true! yet he who does not seek after communion with God through prayer cannot properly understand it."

"Therefore, my fellow-called, if we are desirous of being thoroughly redeemed and sanctified, of living peacefully and dying happily, we must become inhabitants of our own hearts, and fellow-inmates with God. Jesus has opened to us this new and living way in His blood, so that eternal love with its attractions and influences, can now approach very near to us, and we can draw near unto God in our hearts, with childlike confidence, without reference to our misery and unworthiness. Let us then draw near (Heb. 10:22) and freely use this invaluable privilege. Let us accustom ourselves, the whole day long, and even whilst in business, to the Lord's presence, and seek in simple faith to make ourselves known and intimate with Him in our hearts."

Louis Harms

In the 1800's there was another notable German pastor who left his mark upon the spiritual life of his country. Louis Harms was born in the then kingdom of Hanover and traced his pedigree back to one of the three mighty Hermanns, but which of the three he never intimated. A strong spirit ruled an equally strong physical and mental nature.

This German was known for his tenacious faith and the spirit of prevailing prayer which he believed to be vital to any lasting accomplishment in the Kingdom. Like other saints of God, he had known a time in his life when he had yielded body, soul, and spirit to the Sovereign God for His will to be wrought out.

When Louis Harms entered upon his labor for God, a dead orthodoxy prevailed in his area. A visiting minister would be more likely to enquire, "How are your cows?" than to enquire of the state of the soul. The spiritual demands made upon unilluminated ministers irked them, and when asked to make a visit to a sick bed, one replied, "Ach Gott! So I've got to pray again." It was not strange, then, that they would oppose the labors of men who insisted upon the aid of the Holy Spirit in all their endeavors.

Like many another vineyard laborer, Harms was caught in the net of such multiplied duties that time for prayer did not have priority. Once when visiting a Quaker, he recounted his multitudinous responsibilities. The Quaker quietly remarked to him, "Brother Harms, if thou speakest so much, when art thou quiet? When doth the Spirit of God speak to thee?" Harms was deeply impressed and from that time sought to give to each day a certain portion of retirement.

His parish was ten miles square, comprising seven villages, with a population of four thousand four hundred. A thousand at a time would come flocking from these villages to the sanctuary on the Sabbath where they could hear the inspiring messages from Harms' lips. Four hundred would often meet on Wednesday. Drunkenness and poverty were unknown there. Their villages were models of tidiness. Besides preaching, Harms conducted prayer-meetings every evening in his house, and two meetings almost daily for enquires concerning both spiritual and temporal matters.

"Besides all this, with studying and letter-writing, he organized the congregation into a missionary society, sending out their own members to the foreign field; building for themselves a Mission ship, which they kept continually passing from Hanover to the stations in Africa; editing a monthly missionary journal, of which fourteen thousand were published; training the missionaries for their work; and, finally, superintending an establishment for discharged convicts." A peculiar disease which robbed him of sleep provided him with extra time for these colossal labors.

"That which does not anger the unconverted, does not edify the converted," Harms concluded. "What offends not the obstinate cannot awaken the sleeping. That which does not slay, cannot make alive. Bees without stings make no honey."

"His view of prayer and his use of it are strongly exhibited in one of his enterprises. An immense difficulty—impossibility, unbelief would have called it—met him. Thus he describes his course: 'Then I knocked diligently on the dear God in prayer.' Then came relief, and then another difficulty. Of that he thus speaks: 'That was a time of great conflict, and I wrestled with God; for no one encouraged me, but the reverse; and the truest friends and brethren hinted that I was not quite in my senses. I prayed fervently to the Lord, laid the matter in His hand; and, as I arose at midnight from my knees, I said with a voice that almost startled me in the great room, "Forward, now, in God's name."'"

Art thou faint? He stands beside thee;
He shall help thee, guard thee, guide thee;
In His shadow He shall hide thee—
    "Forward, March!"

Through the allurements of temptation,
Through the fires of tribulation,
Holding forth the great Salvation,
    "Forward, March!"

97

By ten thousand foes surrounded,
Mocked, opposed, assaulted, wounded,
Thou shalt never be confounded—
    "Forward, March!"

Till thy bending head be hoary,
Till shall close thine earthly story,
Till thou step from grace to glory,
    "Forward, March!"
                                    —Monod.

Harms enjoyed a constant state of revival for seventeen years. "Hermannsburg rivaled any other community perhaps in the world," stated his biographer, E. N. Kirk, in *Lectures on Revivals.* "Probably not a parish in Christendom equals in spiritual attainment that of Hermannsburg. One writer puts the communicants, in all, at eleven thousand."

Zwemer, in *Taking Hold of God,* says, "Pastor Louis Harms by faith and prayer led the peasants of the Hermannsburg Church to plant the Gospel abroad, so that after thirty-one years he had put into the field three hundred and fifty missionaries and at the end of forty years his mission gathered out from heathenism a church of more than thirteen thousand members."

Bengel

Before the icy fingers of rationalism had gripped Germany in their formal grasp, there were many godly ministers whose lives we can review with some inspiration and benefit. Bengel was one of them. Bengel was born the 24th June, 1687, near Stuttgart. His father, a parochial minister, taught him privately until he was six, but upon his death, David Spindler became the boy's tutor. Bengel's father had bequeathed him his large and valuable library, but when the French invaded that part of the country they destroyed his home and everything in it. Bengel could see God's hand in this loss, for the treasured library would have been a constant temptation to read too much, he being a scholar by nature.

Bengel became revered as a great commentator, and John Wesley's *Notes on the New Testament* were interspersed frequently with his comments on the Scriptures.

"A student of Bengel's, anxious to know the secret of his spiritual power, sat up one night in a room adjoining his study, determined to overlook his last prayer before retiring. At a late hour the venerable scholar closed his Bible and laid aside his manuscripts, and then, without rising from his study chair, he bowed his head over the closed Bible, and said these words: 'Good-night, dear Lord God and Jesus; Thou knowest that we are on the same old terms.' Then he kissed the Book and laid himself down to sleep on a couch."

Tholuck

Tholuck was another German educator who had a profound influence on the students at the university where he taught. Often he would take walks with some of the them, and his conversations were highly prized by these young men—the future manhood of Germany. What he says about prayer shows him to be no mean interpreter of this diligent art.

"If thou wouldst acquire this peculiar kind of prayer which transcends both place and time, thou must begin with the humility of a child to pray at the particular place appointed by God for the purpose, which place is the sanctuary or the silent closet. Prayer is an art and every art requires to be learned with pains. Do not therefore shrink from what may seem to thee the trouble of attending at the time and place God has pleased to assign. All art, however, by slow degrees, becomes at last a second nature; and so likewise, as thou wilt find, does the art of prayer. And when thou shalt have attained to such proficiency, then thou wilt 'neither in this mountain nor in Jerusalem, worship the Father,' but will raise the memorial of His name at any spot on the face of the earth."

MORE GERMAN PREACHERS

John Gossner

The early part of John Evangelist Gossner's life has been included in our book *Opposition,* Vol. 2, of the "Call Back" series. But there we only took up to his 56ᵗʰ year when the true purpose of God for his life was revealed. His good biographer, Dr. Fleming Stevenson, in *Praying and Working,* said of this fresh beginning: "It was now that the work of his life began. He was in his fifty-sixth year, truly a late starting, but he was singular in everything. God had been educating him; and if the foundation was tedious and deep, the building was a glorious temple of the Spirit.

"Few men have had such a training: thirty years of conflict without and within; a continued overthrow of his own plans; the rending of every attachment; persecution and applause; an endless tossing over a stormy sea. No doubt, it was needed; God's children are not tried for nought. He Who is the treasury of wisdom will not let the painful lessons of years be thrown away; and if we see a man cut down before the gathering of the fruit, can we pierce within the veil, or can we count the fruit which angels gather with unseen hands? But Gossner was to have yet thirty years of service; and when he died he was like a tree whose branches bend with heavy ripeness to the very ground."

"Five years since," he wrote to a friend, "I fell—rather was thrown—out of the pulpit. How hard to climb to it once more! Pulpit-stairs are perilous for me to go up and grievous to go down."

Stevenson writes further: "Of scientific theology he had an instinctive dread, lest it should usurp the place of the theology of the heart. 'The scholastics,' he said, 'never opened my eyes; if they did not make me skeptical, they left me just where the false philosophy did.'"

"For some time Gossner remained quietly at his pastoral work, confined often for months to his room by severe pain. There, one day, three or four young artisans came to him. They had been turned away

100

from the seminary as incapable. They burned, nevertheless, to go out among the heathen; they sought his counsel and help. He refused them. They besought him again and again. He prayed for direction and took them. They came—they were now ten or twelve—a few hours every week. 'What shall I do with you? Where shall I send you?' he said. 'I don't know; I can do nothing for you.'

"'Only pray with us,' they replied; 'that can do no harm; if we can't go, we must even stay. But if it is God's work and His holy will that we go, He will open the door in His time.'

"Gossner withdrew ashamed and strengthened; he felt the mission was begun." The story of how he found places of labor abroad for these young men and finance to support them is of itself a long one and we will not go into it here, for this is to show the place that prayer had in this marvelous missionary enterprise begun so late in life.

"Gossner had a prudent and manly horror of reports and statistics as any gauge of success; he took it that the work is for the most part hidden, and is not to be annually dragged up to the light as children do with their first seeds. One day, an old friend, as they sat together in his arbor, asked him how many his missionaries had baptized, and hinted that it was a matter of curiosity among the brethren at the Pastoral Conference. 'So, so,' he replied, 'the gentlemen would like to know. But do not the gentlemen remember a certain king who thought he would number his people and what a sorry ending it had?'

"Yet it may not be out of place to mention that he sent in all 141 missionaries, (including the wives of those who were married, 200,) of whom fifteen were regularly ordained ministers, and 113 are still in active service."

"There is a kingdom into which none enter but children, in which the children play with infinite forces, where the child's little finger becomes stronger than the giant world; a wide kingdom, where the world exists only by sufferance; to which the world's laws and developments are forever subjected; in which the world lies like a foolish, willful dream in the solid truth of the day. Gossner had been brought into that kingdom; these questions were nothing to him; it was enough that he could kneel down and pray. Standing by his open grave, one said of him, and it was not hyperbole—'He prayed up the walls of a hospital and the hearts of the nurses; he prayed mission-stations into being, and missionaries into faith; he prayed open the hearts of the rich, and gold from the most distant lands.'"

"So soon as he came to Berlin, he gathered a few round him for prayer. They continued in prayer while he lived. He could not be present where it was excluded. The Bible Society had determined to open its committee meetings only with silent prayer; he protested, and the protest showed how deeply his heart was sunk in the heart of Christ. 'A Bible Society that does not begin with prayer is to my mind a profane synagogue. . . . I do not despise a short, silent prayer; but it is too little at a Bible Society, and no more than if a nurse said to a child, Make a curtsey, and it made it, and that was all. . . . If I went to the meeting and sought prayer, and it was forbidden, I would take my hat and stick and run out as if a mad dog had bitten me. . . . If I could raise the dead, I would go to Wittenberg and call Luther out of his grave, and Spener, and Arndt, and Andreä, and bring them to the Bible Society at Berlin, and let them decide.'

"That was the spirit in which he undertook the mission; that was the guidance by which it was ruled; and whatever letters, or questions, or threatenings, or difficulties, whatever private or public sorrows reached him from any quarter of the mission-field, they were directly put before God. 'Here I sit,' he would say, 'in my little room: I cannot go here and there to arrange and order everything; and if I could, who knows if it would be well done? But the Lord is there, Who knows and can do everything, and I give it all over to Him, and beg Him to direct it all, and order it after His holy will; and then my heart is light and joyful, and I believe and trust Him that He will carry it all nobly out.'

"He dedicated to this intercourse the latter part of his life; retiring not only from public interests, but from his acquaintances, and incurring the charge of being unsocial and unloving. And he was so guided by the hand of God, and his prayers were so answered, that the universal feeling of the missionaries at his death was, 'Who will now lift up his hands to Heaven in prayer for the scattered children?' And so, almost in prayer, he died; not, however, for the missions alone.

"When he came to Berlin there were no hospitals; there was no visiting of the poor, no inner life stirring in the Church. Germany was just recovering from the paralysis of dead, coarse unbelief, and the materialism of a very false philosophy. For years after, he was a rallying-point for the scattered, struggling, feeble, and despised piety. Home missions also occupied his mind. He established a society for visiting the sick. It was confined to men. The women begged him to form and direct one for them. The necessity of a hospital soon became manifest; and in 1837, a house for forty was erected, and in 1838 enlarged for twenty more. Thirteen deaconesses remained in the hospital; as need arises, some are drafted elsewhere and new candidates supply their place. The training is intensely Christian; the organization just as simple.

"He wrote much to the very last. At seventy he learned English, and translated some of Ryle's tracts when he was upwards of eighty. His writings, at present numbering forty-six, occupy a separate Book and Tract Society; and many volumes of posthumous papers are announced. Those already published possess an unusual popularity, some having run through annual or semi-annual editions for many years. Up till the Spring of 1858, he corrected proofs and continued his correspondence. The summer previous he was still able to train his vines. By the end of March he had fought the good fight and finished the course—a young, old man of eighty-five.

"By faith he preached Christ crucified in the Church of Rome; by faith he resigned his cure in Dirlewang rather than give up one jot of the truth; by faith he lived at Munich, and spread the good news of the kingdom; by faith he went to Petersburg; by faith he was led to Berlin; by faith he sustained the hearts of 100 missionaries, and bore the burden of twenty stations and built an hospital and wrote Jesus upon thousands of lives.

"By faith—by prayer—that is his teaching. He was long in the school, learning and unlearning; it was the time of an ordinary life. But he left it ready for his calling and such a teacher never dies. The tediousness of pupilage is no waste when the workman needeth not to be ashamed. From humble little Hausea and the unnoticed struggles of a country priest to the *Father Gossner* of a reverent, religious Germany; from Feneberg's little parlor and the simple talk of the parish, to the furtherest ends of heathendom and a name that is lovingly spoken on every continent of the globe, is a mighty stride. Neither brilliant talents nor the tide of fortune helped him. Whoever seeks the way to it, will find it to be that plain, old-fashioned one of faith and PRAYER."

Frederick Godet, the commentator whose books are now on the bookshelves of many ministers and laymen, was brought to a saving knowledge of Christ, after his sore conflict, through reading a sermon by John Gossner. What a tremendous out-flowing of influence there is in a godly life of prayer. It lives on forever!

> Since then, these three wait on Thy throne,
>   Ease, Power, and Love, I value prayer so,
> That were I to leave but one,
>   Wealth, fame, endowments, virtues,—all should go:
> I and dear prayer would together dwell,
>   And quickly gain, for each inch lost, an ell.*
>   —George Herbert.

*ell is an old English measurement of one and a half yards.

BOOKS ON PRAYER BY E. F. & L. HARVEY

Kneeling We triumph, Books 1 & 2
Each book contains 60 stimulating readings composed of gleanings from the writings of godly men and women.

Royal Exchange
31 daily readings on prayer.

How They prayed, Volumes 1, 2, & 3
Volume 1 deals with the subject of household prayer, citing many instances of striking answers that have been received.

Volume 2 reveals how godly ministers of the past have had to spend many hours in prayer in order to see lasting results.

Volume 3 shows how missionaries who have done exploits for God and successfully invaded the kingdom of darkness have prayed hard and long. The book also records the mighty praying that has accompanied past revivals.

Asking Father
A book intended for children but which makes excellent reading for adults also. These short factual stories show the wonderful interest and concern of our Heavenly Father Who delights to hear and answer the prayers of His children.

CPSIA information can be obtained
at www.ICGtesting.com
Printed in the USA
BVHW032325050321
601442BV00014B/148

9 781932 774771